TRUE TALES OF THE SUPERNATURAL

& UNEXPLAINED: VOLUME 1

BY

Cindy Parmiter

Table of Contents:

Introduction

Chapter 1: That Thing in the Night
Chapter 2: The Evil Inside
Chapter 3: Forever on the Green
Chapter 4: The Tortured Soul
Chapter 5: The Warning
Chapter 6: Something to Remember Them By
Chapter 7: The Traveling Soldier
Chapter 8: The Dream Man
Chapter 9: A Child's Place
Chapter 10: Only What the Eyes Can See

Epilogue
Acknowledgements
Sources
Copyright

Introduction

We are told from the time we are mere youngsters that there is a logical explanation for every occurrence. Those words of wisdom make perfect sense; if only they were true. We know that scary creatures don't visit us as we slumber in our cozy beds, or remain behind in spirit form long after their physical selves have departed this earth. We know too that otherworldly beings can't warn us of things yet to come. Everyone is aware that objects hold no power over us and can in no way influence the paths we take in life. An individual, racked with grief and guilt, cannot be trapped between the world of the living and the one that awaits them in the beyond. A place meant to be a haven for a woman and her family can't be inhabited by vengeful entities bent on keeping what is theirs at all cost. Indeed, conventional wisdom would have us believe that none of those things are possible. Unfortunately for those who have lived through these nightmares, they are all too real. Their stories, among others, are only a page away. With that said, the time has come to settle in and let the nightmares begin.

Chapter 1:
That Thing in the Night

Historically, the thing that goes bump in the night is the seed from which most horror tales grow. It is something we all fear, even if we are loath to admit it. The mere utterance of the phrase "Did you hear a noise?" can make even the bravest among us catch a quick breath. In the end, there is nothing to fear. It is just the house settling or a neighbor's cat enjoying a midnight snack, courtesy of your trash cans. That is, unless you are the unwitting host to a mysterious night creeper. Such is the story of Allison Walters and the creature she called "The Shuffler."

Allison first shared her experience with me through social media. The events she related were so unique and terrifying that I planned this book around them. If you are someone who fears the darkness and the things that hide within, you might want to skip this one.

In the mid-1990s, college student Allison Walters shared a duplex apartment in Charlotte, North Carolina with her boyfriend, Ryan. It was a decent home in a bustling neighborhood. The couple lived there for nearly a year without incident. It would be on a cold winter's night that Allison would have her first encounter with an uninvited guest.

Allison is not sure of the exact date, but does remember it being sometime after Christmas, 1996. She and Ryan were in bed when she felt a sudden chill in the room. She noticed that the blanket that had been covering them was now at the foot of the bed so she reached down to pull it up over them. The problem was that, when she tugged on it, it didn't want to budge.

Thinking that the cloth was caught on something, she gave it a hard jerk and it finally gave way. As it did, she heard something heavy hit the floor. She also heard what sounded like a small animal scurry across the floor. The couple had no pets at the time. Alarmed, she immediately jumped up and turned on the overhead light.

Ryan stirred and asked what was going on. Allison wasn't sure, but she feared that they had a rat or some other pest in the apartment. She told Ryan what had happened. They searched the room and closet, but could find no sign of whatever had been sharing their blanket that night.

It was still dark outside so there was nothing more that could be done at the moment. Ryan told Allison that he would call the landlord in the morning. That was all well and good, but Allison decided to sleep in the living room all the same. She didn't want to wake up and find a raccoon or squirrel in the bed.

The next morning, they contacted the landlord who said that he would come take a look around the apartment later in the afternoon. Allison was still on break from school so she stayed home to wait for him while Ryan went to work. In the meantime, she performed another, more thorough search of the bedroom, but could find nothing that indicated that an animal was living there. There were no holes in the walls or closet that even a mouse could fit through. She was hoping that he landlord would have better luck finding the culprit.

When the man who owned the property finally showed up late in the day, Allison told him of the night visitor. He searched everywhere he could think of for some kind of evidence that an animal had found its way into the apartment. He even checked the perimeter of the outside of the building, looking for a means by which an animal could enter. Everything seemed secure from what he could see. If something had made its way into the apartment, it had done so without leaving any clues as to how it managed such a feat.

The landlord explained to Allison that none of his previous tenants had ever had any problems. He took care of the building himself and new every inch of it. If there was an infestation of some kind, it would be news to him. He told her to let him know if it happened again and he would call an exterminator, although he doubted that such a measure would be necessary.

Allison didn't sleep well for a while after the blanket incident, still certain that some kind of animal was in the apartment. When night after night passed without a hitch, she relaxed and things returned to normal. Ryan had never really been bothered by it. Only Allison had heard anything that night and he told her long afterward that he thought she had dreamed the whole thing.

It was a week or so later when both Allison and Ryan began noticing that items in the apartment were coming up missing or being misplaced. The first thing that vanished was, oddly enough, Allison's toothbrush.

There was, and had been since they moved in, a toothbrush holder on the sink in the couple's bathroom where they both kept their brushes. Allison always brushed her teeth every morning as soon as she got out of bed. On this particular day, only Ryan's brush was on the sink. Hers had somehow disappeared. She questioned Ryan who swore that he hadn't touched it. Why would he? He had his own.

Even though she knew that she had put her toothbrush back where it belonged the previous night, she convinced herself that she had misplaced it. That being said, it never did turn up. That was just the beginning. Other things started disappearing on a daily basis. They were always items that one wouldn't normally miss. It only became obvious because of the sheer volume of belongings that were being displaced.

Some of the things that the couple noticed were being pilfered were socks, any kind of hair clasp or band that Allison left out, bar soap, the plug from the bathtub drain, pens, pencils, ear swabs and, most annoyingly for Allison, tampons. The couple also noticed that the dish of cough drops that they always kept on the bedroom dresser was often empty, no matter how many times they refilled it. Something was helping itself to random objects around the apartment, but what?

As strange as the goings on in the home were, Allison and Ryan didn't know what to do about it. They hesitated calling the landlord again about the theft. They weren't sure that anyone would believe that someone was sneaking into their apartment to take their cotton swabs and rubber bands. They probably would have let the whole thing go had it not been for what happened next.

Several weeks had passed since the night that Allison had heard something in the bedroom. It was in early February that they were, once again, visited by an intruder. This time, they caught a glimpse of the thing that had taken up residence in their home.

It was sometime in the middle of the night that Allison first sensed something moving about in the hallway. The couple always slept with the bedroom door open to let the warm air in. Their bed faced the bathroom across the hall. The nightlight that burned beside the sink illuminated the bathroom and a portion of the hallway. In the dim light, she could see something walking back and forth between the living room and the bathroom.

Allison lay perfectly still, too frightened to move. It was clear that the thing she was watching was not a squirrel or a raccoon or any other creature she had ever seen before. The size of a small house cat, whatever it was had walked upright on two hind legs. Strangely, although she was aware of its presence, it didn't seem to notice her at all.

Not wanting to alert whatever was in the hallway, Allison nudged Ryan awake. She put her hand over his mouth and motioned for him to look into the bathroom. He, too, saw the thing as it continued moving from one room to the other. At times, it would drop to the ground and walk on four legs. When it did this, they were sure that it was some kind of animal, just nothing they were familiar with. It was when it would rise up and walk on its back legs that they couldn't figure out what it was. It didn't wobble or teeter, but instead walked as comfortably on two legs as it did on four.

Both Allison and Ryan were afraid to say a word. They didn't know if this creature was aggressive and didn't want to find out the hard way. Even though Allison wasn't aware of it at the time, Ryan had a plan. At one point, while the creature was in the bathroom, Ryan jumped out of bed and raced into the hallway. He slammed the bathroom door shut, trapping the night visitor inside.

Allison couldn't believe what had happened. Ryan told her to call the police. He figured that they could contact animal control once they got there. Allison and Ryan listened at the bathroom door as they waited for help to arrive. As much as they tried, they couldn't hear a peep coming from the other side of the door. Whatever this thing was, they had captured it. Perhaps it had given up and accepted its fate.

When the police arrived, Ryan told them that they had trapped some sort of animal in the bathroom. He didn't want to tell them that the thing had walked upright and had been stealing things for weeks. Some things are better left unsaid.

When the officers slowly opened the door, everyone prepared themselves for some critter to come running out in a desperate bid to escape. Instead, there was no movement or sound in the tiny bathroom.

The policemen opened the door all the way and searched high and low, but the room was empty. There was no animal inside, or any other living thing. There were no windows in the room and no visible means of escape. There were also no signs that an animal had ever been there. Nothing seemed to be disturbed. If something had been in the bathroom, it was gone now.

The officers were as perplexed as Ryan and Allison. They wondered aloud if Ryan had only thought that he had trapped something in the bathroom. They suggested that perhaps it had run past him without his noticing.

Feeling more foolish by the minute—and sensing that it wouldn't do any good anyway—the couple didn't argue the point. Nonetheless, Ryan knew that he had closed the door with the thing on the other side. He couldn't explain how it had managed to escape, but he knew that it had.

Although both Allison and Ryan had seen the unusual intruder roaming through their apartment, they didn't want to accept the fact that it could be anything other than some form of wildlife that had found its way into their home. Bound by a lease, they decided to remain in the apartment and deal with the problem. They called the landlord and asked him to contact an exterminator.

They were told that it would be a couple of days before someone could come and inspect the property. Allison and Ryan braced themselves for another encounter with their uninvited guest, but it seemed to have left on its own. They hadn't noticed anything missing since the night they had seen the invader, except for the creature itself.

When the exterminator arrived, Allison explained to him that they had seen a raccoon in their bathroom. She didn't know what else to call it. He proceeded to search the entire apartment for an entryway that was allowing something to access the home. He could find nothing. The man told her that the only options he could offer were to either lay out poison pellets or set a live trap, which he didn't have on hand at the moment. He explained that his field of expertise was in rodent and insect control.

Allison gave him the go ahead to set out poison in various areas of the apartment. However, she felt a twinge of guilt in doing so. They didn't really want to kill the thing. They just wanted it out of their home. Ryan did buy a small live trap at a local feed store and they baited it with peanut butter sandwiches in hopes of catching the creature alive.

Every single night for the next few weeks, they placed the food in the trap before they went to bed. It was set up just outside of the bathroom so that they would hear the door shut if they caught anything.

They checked the trap first thing each morning only to find that the sandwiches were missing even though the trap had not been sprung. Whatever this thief in the night was, it was clever enough to sneak the food out without setting off the sensitive mechanism that controlled the trap's door.

The poison pellets that the exterminator laid out were never touched. Allison made a point of checking them every day and the level never went down. Ryan suggested that they hide the poison inside the sandwiches. On the nights that they tried this bit of trickery, the visitor left the sandwiches untouched.

Items once again began to disappear just as they had before. Again, they were things that no person would ever take. Things like Ryan's contact lens case, any cotton swab that was left out and the small plastic cups that they used to rinse their mouths after brushing their teeth would turn up missing out of the blue. Even though most of the objects taken were placed high up on the sink or even on top of the medicine cabinet, the thief somehow managed to find them and carry them off.

Eventually, Allison and Ryan stopped baiting the trap. They figured that they were just feeding whatever this thing was and encouraging it to keep coming back. They hadn't actually seen their houseguest since the night they locked it in the bathroom. Still, on various occasions, they had both heard something scurrying in the night, which they assumed was the mysterious bandit.

Allison explains that, since they never really knew what they were dealing with, they sort of lost their fear of it. Nevertheless, they started sleeping with the bedroom door closed to keep the thing out of their room. It was never active during the day, so they went about their business with no worries. They didn't bother it, and it didn't bother them.

Going to the bathroom during the night, she admits, was the only loophole in the system. They both feared running into the thing in the hallway or, heaven forbid, while using the facilities. Fortunately for everyone involved, nothing ever happened. The thing in the apartment seemed to know when to make itself scarce.

Allison and Ryan remained in the apartment until their lease was up. In total, they had spent nearly eight months sharing the space with an unknown creature who stole random objects from them, walked equally well on its hind legs or all fours, could outsmart a live trap each and every time, and was able to enter and leave the dwelling by some mysterious means that no one could figure out.

What was the thing in the night that ended up cohabitating with Allison and Ryan? They shared the story with numerous people who all seemed to agree that it was, in fact, a raccoon. It's possible, but why did it take things like bar soap and the bathtub drain plug? What possible use could a raccoon have for such items? Also, how did it manage to escape the bathroom on the night the police were called to the apartment? Raccoons are fairly sizable creatures and no one could find any exit spaces in the room.

Whether the intruder was some type of animal or a creature as yet unidentified, we'll probably never know. You might be wondering if the tenants who moved in after Allison and Ryan had any run-ins with the creature. Unfortunately, that question cannot be answered. They relocated to another city and have no way of knowing what became of their night visitor. It was definitely something unusual and unique in any case.
Whatever it was, it gave a young couple a story they can tell

for the rest of their lives—a story that ends with a question mark.

Chapter 2:
The Evil Within

Holly Young thought that she had found the perfect place to call home when she rented a condo in a nice, quiet area of Salt Lake City, Utah. What she couldn't know at the time was that someone, or something, had already laid claim to the property and they had no intention of sharing it with her or anyone else.

It was in July of 2016 that Holly and her family moved into the quaint, two-bedroom unit. The transition went smoothly, and they settled in with ease. It wasn't long, however, before Holly's partner Teresa began to sense that there was more to the dwelling than met the eye.

Teresa is what some might refer to as a "sensitive," meaning that she is highly intuitive and can pick up on subtle changes in her surroundings that most people never notice. Teresa felt the first inkling that they were not alone in the condo one evening while she and Holly were relaxing in the master bedroom.

Out of the blue, Teresa sensed an energy that enveloped the room. She had a strong feeling that this presence was a spirit who had a connection to Holly. After a brief discussion, the women concluded that it was probably her deceased grandmother paying them a visit.

Even so, since they couldn't be sure who had entered the space, they decided to send it back where it came from using the power of prayer. In the midst of their efforts, Holly says that her grandmother appeared before her.

As she continued to pray, the form morphed into something quite unrecognizable. What had, only a few seconds earlier, been the spitting image of her grandmother was now a dark formidable being, the likes of which neither Holly nor Teresa had ever before encountered.

The women prayed with all their might for the sinister apparition to leave them in peace and it did, but not before scaring the daylights out of them. They agreed that whatever had been in the room that night had not been a lost loved one—as they had at first believed—but rather, an opportunistic spirit that had masqueraded as someone the vulnerable pair would know and trust.

At the time, Holly's sister was staying in the spare bedroom. During her six-week visit, she would also witness the unexplained events taking place within the condo walls. The first episode occurred on the morning following Holly and Teresa's harrowing experience with the unidentified specter.

The women were in the kitchen when Holly began relating the events of the previous night. Without warning, their conversation was cut short by the sound of loud rock music coming from the guest bedroom. There was no one else in the condo at the time and no reason for the ear-splitting music to be playing.

The sisters ran to the bedroom from which the music was emanating. They were shocked to discover that the music was coming from a laptop computer that belonged to Holly's sister. They stopped dead in their tracks when they realized that the laptop was closed and turned off at the time. Holly's sister had to open it and turn it on in order to stop the offending noise. Stranger still, no such song had ever been downloaded onto the device. They had no explanation as to where the song came from or how it had played on a closed laptop with its power turned off.

Shortly after that incident occurred, two dark spots appeared on either side of the bed in the master bedroom. Stranger still, an identical set of prints also showed up in the spare bedroom at exactly the same time. The splotches resembled small footprints and no source for them could be found. Try as she might, Holly could not get rid of the mysterious spots. She utilized all sorts of stain removers and cleansers to no avail. The black footprints remained in spite of all of her efforts.

Holly and her family also began to experience other paranormal phenomena in the condo. Lights would turn themselves on and off at will. Holly's bed moved several inches across the floor by itself. A picture that hung over the bed moved its position on the wall. Doors and curtains would open and close of their own volition. A collection of stuffed animals that Holly kept in the bedroom would be moved to different locations around the room even though no one ever saw who, or what, moved them.

Bizarre noises began to assault their senses, as well. Besides the blaring music, the women would hear someone calling their names at all hours. Holly could sense the presence of someone in her room at night, watching her as she slept. Over time, she would feel the touch of unseen hands on her as she lay in bed, too petrified to move. Whatever was in the room with her, would speak her name over and over throughout the night.

Unexplained odors and aromas also became part of the onslaught of strange occurrences taking place in the condo. At times, perfume would waft through the air. Again, Holly believed this to be her grandmother making her presence known. On other occasions, the acrid stench of rotten eggs would fill the rooms and then be gone in an instant, as if something malevolent had been passing through.

The water in the condo would be perfectly fine one day and putrid the next. The women were constantly on edge, not knowing what to expect from day-to-day.

While every room had its moments, the kitchen seemed to be a hub of activity. The burners on the gas stove would suddenly burst into full-flame for no reason. The blender would turn itself on and off so often that the motor was nearly burned out from overuse.

As the situation worsened, Holly knew that the time had come to seek outside help. In the coming months, she had her home blessed on three separate occasions to no avail. A team of paranormal investigators attempted to cleanse the condo with similar results. Activity would slow down for a short time, but never cease entirely. In fact, after a brief cooling off period, the spirits would return stronger than ever.

During one of the cleansings, the sage that was being used to purify the home refused to stay lit. Finally, it was placed in a deep bowl that sat on the kitchen countertop. The sage was not burning when it was left in the dish.

Holly's sister had taken ill during the ritual and had retreated to her bedroom to rest. Holly was checking on her well-being when they suddenly smelled smoke coming from the kitchen.

What they found could not be explained. The sage was no longer where it had been placed only minutes earlier. Now, although it would not burn during the cleansing, it was ablaze and lying outside of the bowl. The smoke the women had smelled was the sage burning its way through the countertop.

One day, while Holly's sister was in the condo alone, she heard a loud crash in the kitchen. To her, it sounded like pots and pans had fallen out of the cupboard. When she went to investigate, she found nothing disturbed in the room. She did, however, discover a strange red object that had, seemingly, dropped from the ceiling.

No one in the condo could identify the item found in the kitchen that day. It did not belong to Holly or her sister. Keeping in mind the paranormal nature of the activities taking place in her home, Holly buried the object outside underneath a heavy ceramic planter. The destructive nature of whatever they had found became apparent when, within days, the planter began to crumble into pieces.

Holly's sister left the condo shortly after the incident in the kitchen. She had experienced more than her share of strange events during her visit. It was becoming clear that the condo was not a welcoming place for anyone.

It wasn't long after Holly's sister had returned home that new guests arrived. Holly's daughter, son-in-law and six-month-old grandson were the next visitors who would spend time in the condo. Their stay would be brief; with good reason.

Holly set the family up in the master bedroom. Her daughter and son-in-law were spared any firsthand dealings with whatever had infested the condo. The baby, however, would not be so lucky. The infant suffered a night terror that lasted for two hours. Whatever dwelled within Holly's home made it clear, once again, that it didn't welcome visitors. Whether they were adults or children didn't seem to matter in the least.

Family members weren't the only ones who encountered the entities in the condo. Holly had made arrangements to rent out one of her rooms during the annual Sundance Film Festival. It seemed like the perfect opportunity to make a little extra money while providing a safe place for a visitor to spend a few nights. Unfortunately, the unseen inhabitants of the condo had other plans.

The renter arrived as planned and settled into her room. Holly doesn't know what happened after that. Sometime during her brief stay, just after midnight, the woman packed up her belongings and fled the condo. Holly never spoke to her again and has no idea what caused her to beat such a hasty retreat into the night with nowhere to go. She does, however, have a pretty good idea.

At her wit's end, Holly called in a psychic medium in an effort to find out what was haunting her condo. The clairvoyant immediately sensed the presence of more than one spirit in the home. It was determined that some of the entities were relatives of Holly's who had passed on. These beings were friendly and meant no harm to Holly or her loved ones. Unfortunately, they had not come alone.

The medium informed her that there was at least one dark, malevolent spirit in their midst. This sinister presence accounted for the more vile activity in the home, such as the rotten smells and sudden illness. Still, even armed with this new knowledge, Holly was at a loss as to what to do about the ghostly inhabitants. So, with that, the activity continued.

One night, Holly and Teresa were watching television in the living room and discussing a co-worker of Teresa's who had mentioned that she had the feeling that a deceased relative from years gone by was trying to reach her for some reason. This person, she felt, had lived sometime in the mid-1900s.

Just as Teresa was telling the story; Holly's cell phone began to play a song from the 1950s. Not only was it playing the song, but it was manipulating the sound to mimic the staticky tone of an old-fashioned Victrola, despite the fact that Holly had no such function available on her phone.

Holly knew that, in order to live with these constant disturbances, she would have to find some middle ground. She spoke to the spirits directly and laid down some ground rules. She informed them that they could remain in the home, but some areas would be off limits.

For one thing, she didn't want them in her bedroom at night. The feeling that someone was watching her as she slept was becoming too much to bear. For a time, at least, they seemed to oblige. And then, everything changed.

By the end of February, 2017, Holly was busy at work and under more stress than usual. The last thing she needed was to be surrounded by visitors from the spirit world every time she walked in the door. One day, in a moment of sheer frustration, she snapped.

Feeling the whirl of activity around her after a particularly bad day, Holly ordered the entities to go away and leave her alone and they did, but only the benevolent ones. The darker spirits remained and became more vengeful than ever.

The month of March saw an incredible increase in activity in the home. Holly found that the only way she could sleep at night was to listen to church hymns and read Bible scriptures before going to bed. This would allow her a short respite from the onslaught of negative energy that now filled the condo.

Holly returned home from work one day to find that all of her bar stools had been overturned and scattered on the floor. Something was angry with Holly and didn't hesitant to show it.

One night, when Holly returned from the bathroom, she found that the side of the bed that no one slept on had been turned down. On another occasion, the bedside fan she occasionally used had been moved and was running, even though she hadn't touched it.

At times, strange noises would plague her throughout the night. More terrifying still, the bed would shake all night long preventing her from sleeping for fear of what might happen if she closed her eyes.

On the last weekend of March, Holly worked as a volunteer usher for a special event taking place in downtown Salt Lake City; as she had done many times in the past. Exhausted from her long days, she would come home and try to relax by watching some television. Unfortunately for Holly; whatever was haunting her home had other things in mind.

Over the entire weekend, the kitchen lights would turn themselves on and off. When turned on, the lights would glow brighter than they ever had before. On Sunday night, things took an even scarier turn when the spirits began to manifest into something that Holly could actually see.

As she sat in the living room, Holly became aware of dark, shadowy images emerging from the kitchen and swirling their way into the dining room. They were moving along the walls and ceiling as they made their way into the living room. Terrified, Holly sat in disbelief; unable to move.

Realizing the dire nature of the situation, Holly reached for her cell phone and called Teresa. It was she who had given Holly the strength to grab her keys and flee the condo, wearing only her pajamas and a pair of socks. She had been in such a hurry that she hadn't even put on shoes or taken her purse. She was in flight mode and she knew that time wasn't on her side. That would prove to be the last night she would spend in the condo.

Several days later, when Holly returned to collect her things, she noticed large, black splotches on the dining room wall. Teresa was also witness to the odd stains. To the women, it looked as though someone had thrown paint on the walls and then allowed it to slowly creep down to the floor. Appearances aside; this was not paint or any other substance familiar to the frightened duo.

Holly also noticed that a statue of Christ that she kept in the dining room had been turned completely around so that it now faced the wall. She knew that she hadn't moved it and neither had anyone else who lived in the condo.

Not wanting to deal with the hostile entities any further that day, Holly and Teresa left the place they had once called home. They would be back, but this time they would bring along someone who would act as a mediator between Holly and the entities who had succeeded in evicting her.

Fearing for her safety, and that of those around her, Holly called in a medium in an attempt to negotiate with the spirits in the condo. An arrangement was made whereby the women would be allowed four hours each day to clear out their belongings. If they went over the allotted time, there would be hell to pay, literally.

Holly and Teresa realized from the very beginning that this was not going to be an easy task. Four hours passed quickly and they found themselves nearing the cut-off time before they knew it. They soon learned to heed the warnings that were being sent their way when time was coming to a close.

As the fifth hour approached, Holly and Teresa would both notice changes in their own behavior. They would become short-tempered with each other, fighting over insignificant things that normally wouldn't give them a second thought. Once they left for the day, the anger would immediately dissipate and they would have no recollection of what they had fought about or why.

Although they were trying to hurry the process along and get out of the condo in a weekend's time, it wasn't easy. The four hour time crunch wasn't helping matters either. Holly would find herself becoming anxious as the clock ticked down. An oppressive darkness would settle over the condo as the end of the agreed upon time neared. The ordeal also took its toll on Teresa who would become dizzy and physically ill if they surpassed the time limit.

During one of their packing days, Teresa became ill and had to lie down in the back bedroom for a while. As Holly worked in the kitchen, she heard Teresa call out "Hey, honey." When she went to check on her; Teresa told her that it had not been she who had called out. Stranger still, she had heard Holly saying the exact same thing to her at the same time. Whatever was in the condo with them; it had learned to perfectly mimic the women's voices.

In order to hurry the process along and get out of the condo as quickly as possible; Teresa's mother came to help out in the move. She, too, witnessed the strange goings on. Lights would continuously turn themselves on and off. Odd smells would fill the rooms. Doors would open and close. Even when the timeline was adhered to, the spirits made their presence known.

At one point, the women were busy working in the dining room and didn't realize that they had gone over their four hour safe period. They were quickly reminded when a loud bang rocked the condo. The fury was so great that it shook the floor they were standing on. They immediately grabbed their things and fled.

Before Holly was completely moved out, Teresa had a team of paranormal investigators set up an audio recorder and four video devices in a last ditch effort to capture concrete evidence of what was happening in the condo. As this was taking place, a skeptic among them witnessed a stack of boxes begin to shake and move for no reason.

As Holly packed the last of her things and left the residence for the final time, the medium assured her that she would be fine. The main entity that had been tormenting her was attached, not to Holly, but to the condo itself. Closing the door behind her; Holly could breathe easy for the first time in eight months. She was finally free to return to the life she had known before she rented the condo and, unwittingly, stepped into a nightmare.

Not long after Holly moved out, she received an irate call from her former landlord. He was furious with her for leaving the condo in a state of disarray. He informed her that the carpets were soaked with urine and covered in hair. There had been a strict "no pets" policy which he accused her of breaking.

Holly told him that she, nor anyone else who had been in the condo, had any pets. She also let him know that the place had been pristine when she moved out, aside from the black footprints in the bedroom that could not be removed. She had seen to it that the rooms had been thoroughly vacuumed on her final visit. How the carpets got soiled, and who the culprit was, remains a mystery.

In September of 2017, another family was living in the condo. Whether they experienced anything out of the ordinary in their new home, is not known. If they did, they didn't have to endure it for long.

One morning, after the man who had rented the condo left for work and dropped his children off at school, the building caught fire and burned beyond repair. Hearing that there had been a fire, Holly and Teresa drove to the place they had, at one time, called home. Teresa had witnessed the building burning in her mind's eye on the day of the fire. They just needed to see for themselves that it was well and truly gone.

As the couple passed by the condo, one last time, they noticed a sign posted on the front door. Holly got close enough to make out the warning left by the Fire Marshall. It read: "UNINHABITABLE." She couldn't have agreed more.

Chapter 3:
Forever on the Green

There are two golf courses that dominate our local area, one of which is a family owned establishment that has been a mainstay in the community for over seventy years. I have changed the names of those involved in order to protect the privacy of the owners as well as the integrity of their business. Nevertheless, their story is well-known by the locals and for good reason. You see, this particular public course boasts something that most others lack—a resident ghost.

This story first came my way courtesy of an employee who also happens to be a close relative. It seems that almost everyone who has spent any significant amount of time in the country club or on the green has a tale to tell.

No one seems to know exactly when the hauntings began. Some people claim that they have been aware of strange happenings occurring on the property for at least the past twenty years. There doesn't seem to be any one event that grabbed everyone's attention. Rather, this restless spirit tends to prefer making its presence known with a steady stream of whimpers instead of one large bang.

Current employees claim that the vast majority of their encounters with whoever is haunting the golf club occur in the upstairs banquet room. This is an area that is used, on occasion, for parties or business meetings. Otherwise, it is basically a place to store chairs, tables and other items when they are not being utilized.

One male staff member related that he and another employee were given the task of cleaning the banquet room in preparation for an upcoming fundraiser. It was late in the fall and business was slow, so it seemed like the perfect time for such an undertaking.

The two workers gathered up the cleaning supplies and toted them up the stairs. They were the only ones working that day and made sure to leave the door open so that they would be able to hear any customers who entered the restaurant area below.

As they began the arduous job of moving all of the stored furniture so that they could clean the floors, they heard the door at the bottom of the stairs slam shut. One of them went down to open the door, thinking that a golfer might have wandered in and shut the door, not realizing that anyone was upstairs. When the worker tried the handle; the door wouldn't budge. It had been locked from the other side.

The employees began pounding on the door, hoping to get the attention of whoever had locked them in. No one responded to their persistent knocks. They called out to anyone within earshot, but still, no one answered their pleas to open the door.

Fortunately for the workers, there was a back entrance to the banquet room. They had been told not to use the door since it led down some precarious outside stairs that had proven hazardous in the past. Since this was an emergency, they threw caution to the wind and fled down the rickety steps that brought them out into the parking lot.

When the employees re-entered the main lobby through the front door, they discovered that the area was vacant. The restaurant was empty and there were no golfers to be seen. Puzzled, they checked the door that led up to banquet room. To their dismay, they found that it was wide open. They also noticed, for the first time, that it sported a plain knob that had no lock. They couldn't have been locked upstairs, and yet, they had both tried to open the door with no luck. From that point on, they always propped the door open if they had to go upstairs for any reason.

That wasn't the only time that someone had an odd experience in the banquet room. Several staff members claim that they have heard the chairs being moved around when there is no one upstairs. They have also heard the heavy tables being dragged across the floor. When they gather up the nerve to investigate, they find that the room is empty and nothing is out of place.

Employees aren't the only ones who bear witness to unusual occurrences. Occasionally, a golfer will claim that someone was observing them in the locker room. They will be changing clothes when they get the distinct impression that someone is in the room with them, even though the door is closed and no one entered. Most say that they see a figure walking past, only to have it disappear around a corner without a sound. The shaken guest will swear that they were the only ones present in the room at the time.

The kitchen is an area that is frequently targeted by the unseen visitor. One of the staff, whose specialty is food preparation, has been the victim of more than one prank carried out by an unknown perpetrator. The employee, Mark, had his own system for how he laid out the condiments, cutlery, napkins and other necessities. To his great annoyance, someone made it their business to move things around on a regular basis. Still, he didn't let it worry him too much. He was fairly new to the job and assumed that it was someone's way of breaking in the new kid.

Mark first noticed that something was off when he was closing up one night. He had already prepared everything for the following day. The ketchup bottles and napkin holders were filled, cup holders were stocked and tables were cleaned. Everything was in order as he locked up and walked to his car. As he was pulling out of the lot, he noticed that the kitchen lights were still on even though he was certain that he had switched them off before he left. Flustered, he turned around and went back inside.

As soon as Mark entered the room all of the lights went off. He wasn't sure what was going on, but he feared that someone might be inside the building. He turned the lights on and called out to anyone who might be on the premises. No one answered.

Not feeling brave enough to check the entire facility by himself, Mark decided to let it go. He was about to leave for the second time when he happened to glance behind the restaurant counter. It was only then that he became aware that someone had, indeed, been there. He knew this for certain because the napkin holders that he had carefully arranged on each table were now stacked, side by side, on top of the counter. He also noticed that the basket of mustard and ketchup take-a-way packets that he had filled and placed beside the cash register was now under the cabinet where he normally kept the toaster.

Looking around further, he found that the toaster had been moved to a storage cupboard that he rarely used. Someone had definitely been there, and very recently. He quickly checked the cash register and was relieved to find that it was still locked just as he had left it. None of what Mark was seeing made any sense to him.

If there had been an intruder, why had they wasted their time rearranging items in the kitchen while leaving the cash register undisturbed? Besides which, Mark hadn't been out of the building long enough for someone to accomplish what he was seeing.

Not sure what to do, Mark phoned the owner who assured him that it was probably nothing. Mark tried to persuade him to have the police come check the place out, but the owner would have none of it. He ended the call by telling Mark that he would fill him in another time. With that; he hung up. Mark decided that if the owner wasn't concerned, neither was he. He would later find out that his experiences were just the tip of the iceberg.

Unable to shake the feeling that something wasn't right at the golf club, Mark shared his experience with another employee the following day. The woman he chose to confide in was not only a senior staff member, but also a relative of the family who had established the course decades earlier. She told him that there was nothing to worry about. She then opened up to him about their ghost in residence.

The woman, Annie, explained that almost everyone who worked there had seen or heard the ghost from time to time. She told him about the furniture moving about in the banquet room, the toilets flushing when no one was in the restrooms, ledgers coming up missing and later being recovered in empty lockers. Mark's experiences were of no surprise to her since, she informed him, it was common knowledge that the kitchen and dining areas were the favorite haunt of the golf course spirit.

Annie believed that the man who had originally built the business from scratch was the one responsible for the hauntings. He was a distant relative whom she had not known in life, but she did know several of his descendants. Many of them worked, in some capacity, at the golf course. They, too, believed that the man was still around, overseeing the daily operation of the business he had nurtured in life. He was known by all as "Golf Course Pete."

Pete's interest in the golf course didn't end inside the facility. He was also active on the green. The staff who were responsible for making sure all of the golf carts were secured each day at closing would have them lined up and accounted for only to return moments later to discover a stray parked several feet away from the others. No one else would be around and there was no chance that the cart had moved on its own.

The golf course also features a deck on which people can sit and observe the golfers below. Tables and chairs are set up so that those sitting outside can dine as they enjoy the view. This furniture, too, would be moved around as though someone wasn't satisfied with the way it was being displayed. No matter how many times the staff moved them back into their proper positions at closing; they would come in the next day to find them rearranged once again.

Having a ghost on the premises might put some people off, but the employees of the golf course are used to their guest from another realm. To date, no one had ever been harmed in any way. If it is Pete who is haunting the place, he seems only interested in business as usual. Besides the occasional prank, like locking the employees upstairs, he seems to focus on keeping things the way he remembers them. Even on the other side, he apparently likes to keep busy.

Those old enough to remember Pete claim that this type of obsessive behavior fit him to a tee. He was devoted to the business, down to the last detail. He liked things done a certain way and was fairly strict with his employees, most of whom were family.

When Pete wasn't working at the course, he was golfing. It was, after all, his love of the sport that had prompted him to open a club of his own. He had lived his dream. And, it seems that even death couldn't keep him from what he loved most: golf.

For the time being, no one who works at the golf course has any intention of trying to send Pete on to the next life. He seems content there and, as long as he sticks to harmless antics, they plan on letting him be. He worked hard to build a public course for all to enjoy and, at least for now, isn't ready to hand it over to anyone else. The staff is willing to oblige. It is, for them, a family business and Pete—living or not—is still family.

Chapter 4:
The Tortured Soul

The following story is as heartbreaking as it is mysterious. When it was presented to me, it seemed like a tale that should be used as yet another reminder of how fragile our grip on this world truly is and how, in the blink of an eye, our lives can be irreparably altered.

Cheryl Simons grew up in a tight-knit family just outside of Baton Rouge, Louisiana. The numerous cousins, aunts, uncles and in-laws frequently gathered to celebrate birthdays, graduations and holidays. It would be at a fourth of July party in 1991 that she would see the man she knew as "Uncle Rick" for the last time—at least in life.

Rick was Cheryl's uncle by marriage, but she was as close to him as she was to her blood relatives. He was a kind man who doted on his wife and their four children. Looking back now, Cheryl can't think of a time that she had seen him lose his composure or raise his voice above a whisper. It was just the sort of man he was—quiet and unassuming.

When the annual family barbeque ended that evening, most of the relatives said their goodbyes and headed to their respective homes. Traffic would be bad and most of them had a fair bit of driving ahead of them. Cheryl remembers hugging a seemingly endless sea of people as she and her family walked to their car.

She can't recall if she shared a final embrace with her Uncle Rick, it didn't seem important at the time. Everyone assumed that they would all be together again when the next occasion to celebrate rolled around. At least, that was how it should have been but for the merciless hand of fate.

Less than a month after the joyous get-together, Cheryl's family received some terrible news that would leave them shattered. Her Uncle Rick and two of her cousins had been involved in a serious car accident. The trio had gone fishing for the day when, while driving home, they were hit head-on by a driver who had veered into their lane.

Rick survived the crash, albeit with massive injuries. His children, ages eleven and thirteen, were killed upon impact. The family was told that it would be weeks, or even months, before Rick would fully recover. In the end, it would take longer than anyone could have imagined.

The family gathering that occurred this time was a double funeral for the two youngsters who were lost in the tragic accident. Cheryl remembers being in a daze throughout the proceedings as mourners gathered to pay their final respects. Only a teenager herself at the time, it was a surreal experience to see the agonized faces of her loved ones. Everyone was lost in the despair of what had happened so unexpectedly.

Cheryl did not visit her uncle during his stay in the hospital or later when he was moved to a physical rehabilitation center. Although her parents invited her to join them on their trips to the facility, Cheryl couldn't bring herself to face him. She didn't know what to say to someone who had lost so much.

As time went by, Rick eventually recovered enough to return home. Cheryl's mother, whose sister was married to Rick, kept in close contact with the family. Cheryl overheard her parents discussing the situation in what had, at one time, been her aunt and uncle's happy home.

It seemed that Rick's personality had undergone a drastic change following the accident. Even though he had not been at fault, he blamed himself for the deaths of his children. He spoke openly of his wish to die and join them in the afterlife. His wife reminded him that he still had living children who needed him, but his grief was so deeply ingrained, he couldn't hear her.

Other family members, including Cheryl's parents, visited Rick in an attempt to bring him to his senses. They urged him to seek help with his depression. He would listen to them and agree to make an appointment with a counselor. He did not, to anyone's knowledge, ever follow through with his promises. Instead, he sat at home and fell deeper and deeper into an abyss of grief and self-torment.

Cheryl's aunt confided that the Rick who now lived in their home was not the same man she had married. The once kind, soft-spoken gentleman who had always doted on his family and would do anything for anyone was now a tyrant who barely acknowledged his wife or children. If he did speak to them, it was only to yell or curse about some imaginary wrong he felt had been done to him. She found herself avoiding her husband as much as possible. Worse yet, Rick's surviving children told their mother that they now feared and, at times, hated their father.

Rick wallowed in his sorrow for nearly two years until he eventually snapped. He had been an avid hunter before the accident and owned a variety of firearms. Considering his state of mind in the months following the accident, his wife had made a point of hiding the ammunition where she knew Rick wouldn't be able to find it. She had worried more about him harming her and their children than anything else. Her fears would end abruptly one day when, while the kids were at school and she was preparing lunch, she heard a gunshot.

The family was shocked, but not completely surprised, to hear the news that their once beloved Uncle Rick had taken his own life. They were all aware of how much the accident had taken a toll on him. Even though none of them said it out loud, it was almost a relief that his suffering had finally ended.

Again, the tight-knit clan gathered for a funeral. Cheryl couldn't help but notice that her cousins, who had lost their father so suddenly, seemed to be unfazed by what had happened. They had been through a lot in their young lives and their ordeal wasn't over yet.

After the funeral, things seemed to settle down for a while. Cheryl's mother spent a lot of time with her widowed sister. The house that she and her two remaining children lived in was now filled with bad memories so she made arrangements to move to a smaller place in a neighboring town.

She also had other reasons for wanting to move. Cheryl was present on one occasion when her aunt spoke of the strange things that had been happening in the house in the days following the funeral.

On the night after Rick was laid to rest, Cheryl's aunt heard someone crying in the bedroom. She was sleeping on the couch, not wanting to spend time in the room where her husband had died. She assumed that it was one of the children.

When she went into the kid's bedroom to comfort them, she found that they were both sound asleep. Even so, she could still hear someone crying. As she walked through the hallway, she realized that the sobbing was coming from the master bedroom that she had shared with Rick.

As she opened the bedroom door, the crying ceased. She didn't go into the room, even though it had been cleaned and the bed was no longer there. She said later that the room gave her a terrible feeling of anguish. Even walking by it on her way to the bathroom, she would be overcome by such feelings of black depression that she could barely get her legs to move. Once she was away from the room, the dark cloud would lift and she would feel fine. It was just one more reason why she wanted to get out of the house as soon as possible.

The sorrowful crying would become an every night event after the funeral. Cheryl's aunt didn't want to admit it at first, but she knew that it was Rick she was hearing, still caught in the throes of the misery he had endured in life. She noticed other things as well that made her think that her husband was, somehow, trapped in the house. It seemed that, even in death, he had not escaped his dark state of depression.

One of the more terrifying events occurred one evening while she and her children were watching television together. They all heard a ruckus coming from the master bedroom. It sounded as though things were being thrown against the walls with brutal force. They could hear glass smashing as well. All the while, someone was sobbing uncontrollably.

Cheryl's aunt told the kids to sit still while she checked to see what was going on in the bedroom. Under normal circumstances, she would have fled the house, but she was certain that she recognized the cries that were echoing throughout the house. The anguished voice sounded very much like that of her husband, Rick.

As she neared the bedroom door, the familiar feeling of dread washed over her. The room had become a black hole she did not want to enter, but she had no choice. She needed to see what was happening on the other side of the door.

When she entered the room and switched on the light, there was not one object out of place. Nothing was broken. No mirrors or windows were shattered. The room was silent. Even so, the cloistering feeling she had in the bedroom was threatening to suffocate her. She stepped out quickly and returned to assure her children that everything was okay.

A religious woman since childhood, Cheryl's aunt asked the pastor of her church if he would come to the house and say a blessing. She didn't go into all of the details with him. She only told him what she felt he needed to know. The reverend was already aware that Rick had killed himself in the home. She explained to him that she wanted to be sure that her husband's soul could move on. She wasn't certain how he felt about the situation, but the pastor, who was also a family friend, obliged.

Cheryl's aunt walked with him as he blessed the house. It was only when he entered the master bedroom that she saw by his expression that something wasn't right. She could tell, even though he didn't say it, that he also felt the negative energy in the room. He lingered for quite some time, speaking directly to Rick.

The pastor told Rick that he was forgiven of all of his earthly sins and could move on. He then got down on his knees and prayed. Cheryl's aunt knelt beside him and prayed that her dead husband could find the peace in death that he could not attain in life.

It was several months before the family were finally able to move out of the house. The mournful crying could still be heard on some nights, but it didn't happen as frequently after the pastor's visit. Before they moved out for good, Cheryl's aunt took one last opportunity to speak to Rick in the last place he had been before he ended his life.

She stood in the middle of the bedroom and spoke directly to Rick as though he were in the room with her. She told him that he had been a good man and a wonderful father. She assured him that the accident that had taken their children had been unavoidable. It had not been his fault and no one blamed him.

She urged him to move on to whatever awaited him in the afterlife. She told him to take care of their lost children until the time when they would all be reunited. Above all, she asked him to forgive himself.

As one final gesture, Cheryl's aunt asked her children if they wanted to say anything to their father before they left the house. To her surprise, they did. The two youngsters told their dad that they loved and missed him. They told him to go to Heaven and wait for them. With that, what was left of the family said goodbye to the home they had all shared in happier times.

To Cheryl's knowledge, there were no more incidents once the family moved to their new home. Her aunt remarried several years later to a man whose personality was very much like that of her Uncle Rick before the accident. Everything seemed to have come full circle and a family once awash in misery, once again knew happiness.

As for what became of the house where Rick died, its sale was finalized shortly after the family moved out. Cheryl's aunt did note that the oppressive feeling in the bedroom seemed to have lifted after she and her children made their peace with Rick.

They hope that it allowed him to move on. Perhaps, their love and forgiveness finally freed his tormented soul.

Chapter 5:
The Warning

It takes a special kind of person to devote themselves to the care of the elderly. Beth Thompson was one of those people. She always thought of herself as someone who would do anything for her patients. That is, until she came upon one who would leave her questioning, not only her chosen profession, but also her sanity.

Beth had worked as a certified nurse's aide for several years at a home for the aged in Parkersburg, West Virginia. She had encountered her fair share of both kind-hearted patients as well as those whom she could never seem to please. It went with the territory, so she accepted that everyone wasn't going to be happy with what their lives had become.

It was in the late 1990s that a resident who would test Beth on a regular basis entered the facility. The lady was in her eighties and was no longer able to live at home. Her daughter had been the one who had accompanied her on the day she was first admitted. It would be one of her only visits that Beth can recall.

The woman's daughter told the workers who were present that day how difficult her mother was. She explained that she had always been a mean, callous person who only cared about herself. She even used a five-letter expletive to describe her. Beth was surprised at the daughter's candor and the fact that she didn't hesitate to say these things while her mother was present in the room.

None of the workers paid too much attention to what the daughter was telling them. Family squabbles were nothing new to them. They felt certain that this was no different than any other situation they had seen throughout the years. There would be an adjustment period and then things would settle into a new normal for the elderly woman. It would work out. These things always did, or so they thought.

From that first day, until the day that Beth resigned from her job, the new patient made her life a living hell. It became apparent to the staff right away that the daughter had not been exaggerating. Their new resident was exactly as she had been described.

The woman, who we'll call Gladys, lashed out at anyone who approached her for any reason. She refused to participate in any events at the home. She wouldn't go to the dining area at mealtime even though she was able to walk, unassisted. Instead, she chose to sit alone in her room day in and day out. If anyone on the staff suggested she leave the room, she would assault them with a barrage of words not fit to print.

The lady who shared the room with Gladys was also witness to her roommate's bad temper. She would tell the staff that Gladys would sit in a chair by the window and glare at her for hours on end. Making people uncomfortable seemed to give her great pleasure.

Beth knew that Gladys suffered from a liver disorder that caused her stomach to be horribly bloated. Although she was small in stature, her belly resembled that of a woman about to give birth to twins. She also had a yellowish tint to her skin, also indicative of a liver ailment. Gladys complained constantly of how painful her condition was. Beth tried to be sympathetic, but her patient's foul disposition didn't make it easy.

Gladys also seemed to enjoy insulting the staff at the home. She had a disdain for anyone who was overweight and would not hesitate to lay into any nurse or aide who was carrying a few extra pounds. Beth herself had been the victim of her name calling on more occasions than she could count.

One day, after months of putting up with the verbal abuse, Beth snapped. It was bath time and it was her turn to take Gladys down the hall to the shower. This never went well, but on this particular day, the elderly woman was more determined than ever not to go. Gladys never liked to leave her room and almost always refused her shower. She would then complain loudly to anyone who would listen that she wasn't getting bathed regularly.

Even though this had happened many times before, on this occasion, Beth lost her patience. When Gladys lay in the bed and pulled the blanket up over her in an act of defiance, Beth uncovered her and told her that she smelled bad and needed to take a shower. This made Gladys, who was constantly insulting the staff, furious. It was clear that she could dish it out, but she couldn't take it.

The next thing Beth knew, Gladys sat up in bed and grabbed her by the hair with both hands. The elderly woman was surprisingly strong and it took all of Beth's strength to get away from her. When she finally broke free, she could see strands of her hair still clutched between the old woman's fingers.

Although Beth didn't want to lose her temper with a patient, she couldn't stop herself. She clenched her teeth and told Gladys that her daughter was right. She was an expletive. She says that she will never forget the expression on the old woman's face at that moment. The hatred in her eyes was palpable.

It was at that moment, Beth's hair still clinging to her hands, that Gladys uttered a few simple words that would impact the young nurse's aide for a long time to come. Her eyes blazing, she spit out the words: "Just you wait, lady. You're not dead yet."

Beth didn't know what the words meant, at the time. They didn't make sense to her given the situation. Understanding would come later, the hard way.

Following the incident on shower day, Beth tried to avoid being Gladys' caregiver. She didn't like losing her temper with anyone, much less a patient. Beth prided herself on doing her best for those in her charge and, since her interactions with Gladys were unpleasant, she asked to be assigned to another unit in the facility.

To her relief, her request was granted and she wouldn't have to deal with her least favorite patient ever again. She was hoping that this would be the end of it, but as it turned out, it was only the beginning.

It was several weeks after Beth had moved to the rehabilitation unit that she began noticing a dull pain in her abdomen. It would come and go, especially at night. Assuming that it would go away on its own, she didn't give it much thought.

As the days went by, the pain began to occur more frequently. Even more alarming was the fact that her belly was swelling, so much so that her clothes no longer fit properly. Worried that something was seriously wrong, Beth made an appointment with her doctor. She had to find out what was causing this sudden onslaught of symptoms.

Beth's physician could find no obvious cause for the pain and swelling that she was experiencing. He was, however, concerned about her condition. He told her that the whites of her eyes were tinged with yellow, a sign of jaundice. This was a symptom that Beth hadn't been aware of. Now, she was truly worried. A battery of tests was scheduled for the following week. All she could do, for the time being, was to wait and wonder.

It would be weeks before all of the test results came back. When she met with her doctor to discuss the findings, she learned that it had all been for nothing. Judging by the data before him, the doctor could find no explanation for Beth's symptoms.

He explained that her liver was functioning normally, as were her other organs. Her blood work came back normal, even better than normal in some areas. She was a perfectly healthy woman, if the tests were to be believed.

Beth was beside herself. She is embarrassed to admit that she wept when she heard the results, not from happiness but, from frustration. Perfect test results or not, she was getting sicker by the day. Her stomach was so bloated that it was uncomfortable for her to even sit down. She felt as though she would pop at any moment.

The doctor assured her that he wasn't finished yet. They would work on treating the symptoms. It was all they could do given the fact that they could find no medical reason for her condition. The implication was that it was all in her head. Even though he didn't say it outright, Beth knew what he was thinking.

The course of action was to put her on a regimen of several medications and supplements that were designed to rid her body of excess fluid and fortify her liver and pancreas. The treatment did give her a bit of relief, but not much. She was still terribly bloated and her skin was beginning to develop a yellowish hue.

It was around this time, when she could hardly recognize herself in the mirror that she began to wonder if her run-in with Gladys had been the cause of the misery she was now enduring. She hadn't wanted to admit it before, but her symptoms were mimicking those of the elderly woman's to a frightening extent.

She wondered if whatever ailment Gladys had was contagious. After checking with the charge nurse at the nursing facility, she learned that this was not a possibility. Gladys was suffering from cirrhosis of the liver which was not communicable. Besides which, no other staff members had shown any of the symptoms that either of the women were exhibiting.

Still, the thought nagged at Beth. She couldn't shake the feeling that Gladys was somehow responsible for her current situation. She decided that there was only one way to find out and that was to speak to the patient herself. She dreaded the encounter, but needed to find out if Gladys had brought this upon her.

When she finally mustered up the nerve to talk with the old woman, she found her lying in bed and quite docile. Beth asked if she could speak to her for a minute and Gladys nodded her head, but not before thoroughly looking her up and down. After giving her the once over, she appeared to be quite satisfied with the change in the young aide's appearance.

Beth asked Gladys, point blank, if she had anything to do with what was happening to her. Gladys didn't admit or deny anything. She only turned her head and stared out the window.

Beth didn't know what to do. She truly felt that Gladys was responsible, even though she knew it was a ridiculous notion. Even so, her fear and anxiety got the better of her and she burst into tears. "I don't deserve this," was all she could say.

The answers that she had hoped to find were not forthcoming, so she wiped her face with some tissues and turned to leave. Gladys didn't say anything or acknowledge her any further. More disappointed than anything else, Beth left the room. She decided, then and there, to fight with all she had to regain her health.

The same day that she confronted Gladys, she gave two weeks' notice to her employer. With the help and support of her family, she was going to take some time off to focus on getting better. She knew that she wouldn't be able to work much longer if her health continued to decline. It was better to leave now before she got any worse.

Beth then embarked on a routine designed to strengthen her mind and body. She took up yoga and consulted with an herbalist who suggested some natural remedies that would put her on the path to good health. To be on the safe side, she continued taking the prescribed medications as well, leaving no stone unturned in her efforts to get well.

After several weeks of diligence, she started noticing some positive results. The yellowish tint to her skin was beginning to fade. The whites of her eyes were no longer discolored. Best of all, the swelling in her belly had gone down considerably. She could now fit into clothes that she hadn't worn in months.

Beth was still seeing her doctor, who found her progress encouraging. Even though she was doing better than expected, he still suggested that they run a few tests to check her liver functions. Once again, all of the scans came back clean. Against all odds, her condition was improving by the day.

It took nearly six months for Beth to be completely back to normal, physically anyway. She felt, and looked, better than ever. Whatever had plagued her seemed to be gone now. She was even ready to go back to work.

When she returned to her old job, she was welcomed with open arms. She had always been a reliable, hard-working employee and they were happy to have her on staff. It wasn't long before she settled back in to the work routine. She was stronger than ever, in more ways than one.

Beth had been back to work for several weeks when she decided to look in on some of her former patients in the long term care unit. The ones who remembered her were thrilled to see her. A few had passed away, which was not uncommon in the facility.

Although she hadn't made any special effort to visit Gladys, when she passed by her room one day, she noticed that her name was no longer on the door. When she asked the nurse at the desk what had happened to the patient who had occupied bed two, she was told that she had died several months earlier.

While she certainly wasn't happy to hear the news, neither was she sad. If she felt anything at all, it was relief that she would never again have to face the woman who she believed had caused her such misery.

Later on, while Beth was in the lunch area talking to some of the other aides and nurses, she happened to bring up the subject of Gladys. The resident was well known to staffers, mainly because she had been so difficult to deal with.

It was then that she learned that Gladys had died in April. Beth immediately took notice of the time line, mainly because it had been in April that her health had begun to show drastic improvement. Once again, she wondered if the two things were somehow connected.

Beth no longer works at the facility. She is now a private nurse in patient's homes. She loves her job and the people in her care. Even so, she never forgot the incident with Gladys or its aftermath. She couldn't shake the feeling that the old woman's veiled warning had caused her to experience the same symptoms as her patient. Perhaps it was all just a series of coincidences, perhaps not.

Even though she is thankful that everything worked out in the end, Beth still wonders if the symptoms went away because of her commitment to getting well or if the combination of medical and natural remedies cured her. She is also aware of one other possibility.

Could it be that Gladys had afflicted Beth with the same symptoms she was suffering from, only to feel sorry for her actions and lift the curse in her final moments on earth? Or, is it more likely that Beth was so traumatized by her violent encounter with the belligerent patient that she had brought the symptoms on herself? I'll let you be the judge.

Chapter 6:
Something to Remember Them By

When someone close to us passes away, we always hope that they will give us some sort of sign that they are at peace in the afterlife. Sadly, our wishes aren't always fulfilled. Maybe the gesture doesn't come at all or, if it does, we miss it as we get on with our lives. There are those times, however, when those left behind are sure that their loved ones have left their calling card from the great beyond. These are just a sampling of the many stories I have received on this phenomenon.

A lady named Carmen Ball shared this account of the contact she had with her mother after she passed in 2015. Even though her mom had been in poor health for several years, she had not been suffering from anything life-threatening. Her sudden passing had shaken the entire family and all of the people who had known her to their core.

Carmen makes no secret of the fact that she had not always had a great relationship with her mother. They went through a long period of barely speaking to each other when she left home at seventeen to live with a boyfriend. Time passed and, with it, so did the hard feelings between them. In the last few years of her mother's life, Carmen had been the person who had been there for her when others had not.

After her mother's death, Carmen was in charge of settling the estate since she was the closest living heir. Her older brother had been killed in an automobile accident as a teenager leaving her an only child. That one event, more than any other, had sent the remaining family members into a tailspin that would, eventually, tear them apart.

Carmen's parents split up less than a year after her brother was killed. She lost contact with her father several years ago and isn't sure, to this day, if he is living or dead. She holds no ill will towards him for leaving. The grief that had rested heavily upon the household, at the time, was more than anyone could bear.

For her, the worst part was how her mother would lash out at both her husband and daughter for the boy's death. In her misery, she would tell them that she would trade their lives to have her son back. Carmen didn't want to leave her mother, but it had all became more than any teenager should have to endure. She soon took the same path as her father and left the house, and her mother, behind.

This was all, of course, in the past and the two had made their peace with it long before Carmen's mother was laid to rest. They had shared many good times together in the years since they had agreed to let bygones be bygones. The guilt that Carmen had once felt for leaving home had disappeared. She had been there for her mother in the end and that was what mattered now.

Since she had no desire to take over ownership of the family home, she decided to clear it out and put it up for sale. It wouldn't be easy. Her mother had lived there for decades and the place was filled with not only memories, but all of the other items a person collects in a lifetime.

Carmen was not alone in her task. During the time that she was estranged from her mother, she had given birth to a baby girl. The child, now in her twenties, is not only Carmen's pride and joy but, also, her best friend. Her daughter was by her side as she sorted through the multitude of reminders of the past.

As she and her daughter meticulously went through all of her mother's personal items, they kept things that they felt had meant something to her mom. They saved family photos, jewelry, keepsakes and anything to do with her deceased brother. One item, in particular, caught their eye.

It was a small nugget of some kind that had been placed in a jewelry box. Neither one of them could figure out what it was, but they kept it anyway. They figured that, if it had been important enough to be kept in a fancy velvet box, it must have been valuable in some way.

Afterwards, Carmen invited her mother's other relatives and people from her church to come in and help themselves to anything they wanted. She was just going to donate the remaining items anyway and she felt that her mother would want things to go to people she had known in life.

For some reason, she couldn't get the strange object that they had found in the jewelry box out of her mind. It didn't really look like anything, but it nagged at her all the same. She put the box in her purse and decided to ask around to see if anyone else could figure out what it was. It would be a co-worker who would finally solve the mystery.

When Carmen was showing the nugget around during her break at work, one of the men at the table knew exactly what it was. To her astonishment, he told her that it was a gold filling for a tooth. She was pretty sure that her mother had never had a gold filling. The woman had worn dentures for as long as she could remember. Why she had held on to the filling and who it belonged to were secrets that she had taken to the grave.

Carmen's daughter had also been curious about the item. When Carmen told her what it was, she ordered her mom to throw it away. To her, it seemed simple. The filling had been in someone's mouth at some point and it was, in her words, "disgusting."

Even though it had, apparently, meant something to her mother, Carmen had to agree. Once she knew what the object was, it had lost all of its intrigue. She thought it would be strange to take a filling to a gold dealer and try to sell it, so she opted to do just as her daughter had suggested and pitch it. She ended up throwing the filling--box and all--away. Once the deed was done, she didn't give it another thought, that is, until the unexplainable happened.

Carmen was digging around one day in the kitchen drawer she used to hold all of the things that she didn't have room for anyplace else when she made an unusual discovery. As she searched through the random items, she saw something that made her do a double-take. There, among the pencils and paper clips, was the gold filling.

She couldn't believe what she was seeing. It couldn't be, but it was. The box was gone, but the discolored nugget was there before her eyes. She picked it up and immediately phoned her daughter. When she told her about the find, she was stunned to learn that she wasn't the only one witnessing the impossible.

After an excited Carmen finished her story, her daughter informed her of her own, similar experience. She said that had found the nugget in her medicine cabinet one morning when she went to brush her teeth. She had noticed it sitting alongside the toothpaste and lotions as soon as she opened the cabinet door. It didn't belong there and she had no explanation for how it had found its way into her home since she had never had it in her possession.

Carmen asked her daughter why she hadn't told her about finding the filling. Her daughter couldn't say for sure. She had known that her mother had thrown it away. There was no way to explain how it was now in her medicine cabinet. The whole situation was so unreal that she had chosen to pretend that it hadn't happened.

So, instead of telling her mother, she attempted to flush the filling down the toilet. No matter how many times she tried, it wouldn't go down. She ended up fishing it out and throwing it in the trash can. That would be the end of the filling, or so she thought, until it turned up at Carmen's house.

Neither of them could explain how the filling ended up in their homes. Carmen knew, without a doubt, that she had thrown it away, box and all. She lived alone at the time and there would have been no logical way that it could have found its way into her junk drawer. And, yet, she had seen it with her own eyes.

Her daughter's situation was even more bizarre given the fact that the filling had never been in her possession. How it had managed to end up in first one home and then another after being thrown out was a mystery that left them dumbfounded.

The only thing they could think of was that her mother had been leaving it for them to find. As unlikely as that scenario seemed, it was the only thing that made sense. They concluded that, whatever the gold filling had represented to Carmen's mother, it was something that she didn't want to lose. Sensing this, Carmen decided to hang on to the nugget. She felt that it was one last thing she could do for her mom.

Carmen keeps the filling in a trinket box along with her mother's jewelry. She still doesn't know why her mom chose to fixate on this one object. She does believe, however, that it was being used to keep them connected. Perhaps her mother knew that it was something that would capture her daughter's attention. If that was the case, then she was right.

As a footnote, Carmen and her daughter tried to find out who the filling had once belonged to. They asked some of the relatives if they knew of anyone who had ever had a gold filling. None of them did. They were emphatic that it had not belonged to any of them. Carmen has never been able to figure out why someone would give her mother a tooth filling. More to the point, she can't understand why it meant so much to her mother.

At any rate, once in a while Carmen will look through her mother's belongings as a way of remembering her. The filling is always the first thing that catches her eye. Because of it, she will always have a story to tell.

Much like Carmen's experience, Judy Santer also received a gift from someone who had passed on. This time, it was her beloved father who left her a reminder that he would always be with her, in one way or another.

Judy was the only child of Gerald and May Santer. Her father was already well into his sixties when she was born. Having an older father had never been an issue for Judy. Gerald had always been in good health and had played an active role in her life from day one. She adored him and he doted on his little girl.

When Judy was in her late twenties, her father was felled by a massive stroke. He passed away only hours later, his wife and daughter at his bedside. She had always been a daddy's girl and the loss was tremendous. To make matters worse, it was left up to her to make the funeral arrangements.

She remembers seeing him in his casket at the funeral home. To her, he seemed to only be sleeping. She was afraid to look at him at first, but found comfort in seeing him resting peacefully. After she said her last goodbyes, she spent the rest of the day comforting her mother and the other mourners.

As time when by, life returned to a kind of normal, even though Judy and her mother were still grieving the loss of Gerald. Judy says that she often sensed that her father was still present in the house. Sometimes, she half expected to see him sitting in his reclining chair, reading or taking a nap.

A few things occurred that added to the suspicion that the family patriarch was not ready to depart just yet. Gerald had, for as long as she could remember, smoked one cigar every evening after supper. It was his only vice and something he seemed to enjoy immensely.

They began to suspect that something was up when, in the days following the funeral, the aroma of cigar smoke would waft through the house on most evenings. At first, Judy and her mother assumed that it was just wishful thinking, but they soon came to the conclusion that Gerald was still there, at least, in spirit. Rather than being alarmed by the thought, they took comfort in his nightly visits.

About a month after Gerald had been laid to rest, the smell of cigar smoke suddenly ceased. The women had come to look forward to smelling the familiar odor that reminded them of their lost husband and father. For whatever reason, it was over now. They assumed that Gerald had moved on to whatever awaited him in the afterlife.

Judy had lived at home well into her adulthood. As much as she loved her mother and wanted to always be there for her, she decided to finally get a place of her own. She moved into an apartment that was only a few minutes away from the family home. This way, she could check in on her mother daily. It was an arrangement that worked out well for both of them.

It was when Judy was unpacking one of the many boxes she had brought with her from her old room that she came upon something she could not explain. There, amid the various objects she had collected in her life, she found her father's spectacles.

Gerald had always sported an old-fashioned pair of glasses with thin earpieces that curled around the sides of his head. They reminded Judy of a Norman Rockwell painting and she had always loved the way they looked on her daddy.

As memories came flooding back, Judy couldn't help but wonder how she came to be in possession of the glasses. She was certain that her father had been wearing them at the funeral home. He only took them off when he was sleeping or taking a bath. She thought that, perhaps, the people at the funeral home had removed them. Judy wasn't sure, but she decided to ask her mother the next time she saw her.

When Judy told her mother about finding the eyeglasses in her belongings, the woman was more than a little bit surprised. She distinctly remembered Gerald wearing them at the viewing. She hadn't brought them home with her and assumed that he would be buried in them.

Curiosity got the better of them and they decided to phone the funeral home that had taken care of Gerald to find out what their protocol was concerning eyeglasses. The man Judy spoke with explained that they abided by the wishes of the family.

Whether or not someone was buried in their glasses was up to the surviving loved ones. This is all usually discussed up front, he told her.

Judy, nor or mother, could recall being asked about whether or not they wanted the eyeglasses to be interred with Gerald. She realized that they were so distraught at the time that it was possible they had just forgotten all about it.

After speaking with the funeral director, Judy didn't know much more than she did before. Even if her father had not been buried in his glasses, she had not taken them. Her mother also had no memory of having been given the glasses at any time during the viewing or, later, at the funeral. She remembered everything else, but had no recollection of such an event ever occurring.

Judy can't explain how she came to be in possession of her dear father's spectacles. How they managed to turn up during her move, in a cardboard box filled with various other objects, without so much as a scratch on them, she can't say. She hopes that they were left there by her kind and generous father as a reminder that his love was strong enough to transcend anything, even his passing on to places, as yet, unknown.

This final story involves the unbreakable bond a pet owner shares with their animals. I have heard dozens of these heartwarming tales over the years and have included several in previous books. The following account caught my attention right off the bat for it is a perfect illustration of the eternal connection between humans and their most loyal of friends.

Zach Sims and his dog, Bella, had been inseparable companions since he was a child. The yellow lab had joined their family when Zach was only eleven-years old. Even though she was meant to be a household pet, the puppy chose Zach as her person on the first day that his parents brought her home. And so it would remain, until her last day with them, that Zach was the one she loved the most.

All through his teenage years, Zach always had someone to talk to when he couldn't confide in any of the people around him. Bella would watch him through the living room window every morning as he left for school and she would be waiting at the door for him each afternoon when he returned home.

His mother would say that time stopped for the dog anytime Zach was out of the house. He was her whole world and she would stand sentry for hours on end until her boy was back where he belonged.

As Zach grew older, so did Bella. The years ticked by and, although her hips began to give her some trouble, Bella would still play catch with him in the backyard almost every day. Most of the time, she would just lie on the bed beside him while he played video games. No matter what activity Zach was engaged in, it mesmerized his biggest fan. She was always content to be by his side.

When he graduated from high school, he chose to attend a community college rather than move someplace where he would have to live in a dorm. He had several reasons for making this decision and one of them was Bella. He wasn't ready to leave the family behind just yet and that included his most loyal friend.

Zach graduated from college with a two-year degree. It was enough to get him an entry level position as a legal assistant at a local law office. He soon found that he loved the work and thought that, in time, he might continue his education and become a lawyer.

Although his work required him to put in long hours on some days, Zach could always count on Bella to greet him when he returned home in the evenings. He was still living with his parents as he saved money for the future. The arrangement worked out well for everyone involved, particularly Bella. But, alas, all good things eventually come to an end.

He was at work one day when he received an urgent phone call from his mother. She told him that Bella had begged to go outside so she had let her out into the back yard. When she went back to call the dog into the house, she found Bella lying beside the fence. Something was very wrong and she didn't know what to do.

Even though Zach was exceptionally busy, he dropped everything and headed home. He didn't even take time to explain to his co-workers what was happening. He simply told them that there was a family emergency as he rushed out the door.

When he arrived home, he went straight to the backyard. He ran to the spot by the fence where his mother was crouched over Bella. He could tell by the expression on her face that the news was not good.

Zach knelt down and put his hand on the dog's head. Bella's eyes were half-open, but there was no life left in them. He wept, as did his mother, at the realization that his companion of over a decade was gone. He doesn't know how long they sat in the backyard stroking the big dog and saying their goodbyes. It could have been minutes or hours. Time had stood still for them as they grieved the loss of their dog.

The family had Bella cremated so that they could bury her ashes in the yard she had played in since she was a puppy. Zach, especially, wanted a place where he could go and talk to his dog, just as he had done since he was a boy. It gave him some comfort to know that she would always be near him, at least in this one way. He would soon come to believe that she was closer than he thought.

On the night after Bella died, Zach had the first of many experiences that made him think that Bella might still be with him. He had gotten up to use the bathroom sometime during the night when he tripped over something lying on the floor.

Even though she had normally slept with him, there were times—especially during the summer—when Bella would lie beside the bed instead of on the mattress. Zach had accidentally tripped over her in the past, so he knew the feeling. When it happened this time, he told himself that it was impossible since she was no longer there. Still, it had seemed all too real. He had even felt her fur against his bare feet.

That would prove to be the first of many times that Zach would bump into his sleeping dog in the wee hours of the morning. There would also be nights when he would feel her body snuggled up against his as he slept. The sensation was so real that he would reach his hand out to pet her only to find nothing but air. Still, he knew that she had been there, even if he couldn't see her.

His mother also felt that Bella might still be in the house, at least in spirit. She told her son that sometimes after he had gone to work, she would see the curtain moving in the living room, just as it had done for years when Bella would part it to watch her favorite person anytime he left the house. She also shared in Zach's experience of stumbling over a large, furry object in the floor from time to time. It was a bit unsettling, but she had gotten used to it after a while.

The family that Bella left behind also found little reminders of her lying around the house for some time after she died. They had buried a few of her very favorite toys alongside her ashes. Those included the things she loved most in the world, aside from Zach: her much-used tennis balls.

Not all of the yellow balls had been buried with Bella, so no one thought much of it when they would find a stray one underneath the dining room table or laying in the yard. It was after they had collected the last of them that they began to wonder where the never ending supply of tennis balls was coming from. They never did figure it out.

Zach ended up keeping one of the tennis balls for himself. It represented a pleasant memory of the times he spent in the backyard, throwing the ball over and over again for his dog. He still has the toy to this day and considers it one of his most prized possessions.

Bella's presence in the house had become something very real for Zach. She made herself known to him almost every day. She had always, since she was a puppy, scratched and whined at the bathroom door anytime he shut her out. This continued even after she passed.

There were times that he would be taking a shower and hear the familiar whimpering coming from outside the door. He would shut the water off and listen as his dog tried to get into the room with him. When he opened the door, the room was silent and empty. Still, he knew that Bella had been there, if only in spirit.

By this time, Zach had become an integral part of the legal team he worked for. He had done well for himself and was content, for the time being, to continue on as a full-time legal assistant. He had saved enough money to move out and start his life away from the home he had grown up in. His parents had never pushed him to leave. They wanted him to make the decision on his own and he had. The time had come to move on.

What Zach didn't expect, was that the visits from Bella would stop once he moved into his own place. Perhaps it was because she had never been there during her lifetime or, maybe, she decided it was time to let go. At any rate, he didn't feel her presence in his new place.

Zach visited his parents frequently, but found that he no longer had any sense of Bella in his old home, either. His parents, likewise, told him that they hadn't had any experiences that led them to believe that the dog was there once he moved out.

The family all believe that Bella stayed with them for a while after she left her physical body. They had all sensed her presence at different times. They aren't sure why she chose to move on when Zach left home, but they have a theory.

Since Bella had always been there for Zach, the family feels that she stayed around long enough to see him settle into his life as an adult. Once he had moved out and begun a life of his own, she chose to move on also. She job there was complete. She had watched over her boy until he no longer needed her.

Even though he misses her every day, Zach has made peace with the fact that Bella is no longer with him. He even has another dog now, something he thought would never happen.

His new companion, however, was never meant to replace Bella, who was special in so many ways. As they say, the worst part of owning a dog is saying goodbye. Bella, somehow, made even that a little bit easier for the ones she left behind.

Chapter 7:
The Traveling Soldier

This story was contributed by Margaret Shields who grew up, along with her brother Bob, just outside of Flint, Michigan. They fought and bickered, as siblings tend to do, throughout their childhoods. Still, they were always there for each other through thick and thin. They had a bond that even death could not break.

Margaret, known as Margie to her family, remembers well the turbulence of the 1960s. She, and her brother, knew that a war was brewing in a place called Vietnam, but it seemed very far away and nothing for them to be worried about. They lived their lives, enjoying their teenage years to the fullest, while many of those around them readied themselves for the years of turmoil they sensed were about to paralyze the country.

Although the Shields' youngsters didn't keep up with current events at the time, their parents did. Margie began to notice that the conversations at dinnertime soon shifted from the humdrum subjects of work and school to the possibility of war.

Mr. Shields, in particular, seemed to be obsessed with what it would mean for their family. Margie didn't realize, at the time, that her father was thinking ahead to the likelihood that Bob might end up fighting a war on foreign soil.

Bob, for his part, didn't seem too worried about his future. He knew what he wanted to do with his life and nothing, not even the possibility of war, could sway him. Bob was going to be a professional musician and that was that.

The teenager had taught himself how to play the guitar when he was barely big enough to hold the instrument. Everyone marveled at his natural ability. He was talented and he had no plans to let it go to waste. When he wasn't in school, he was practicing the guitar, honing his skills for the career path he had chosen.

Time ticked by and the United States eventually entered into the conflict in Vietnam, just as many had feared. By the early 1970s the Shields' siblings had both graduated from high school and were taking steps towards their respective futures.

Margie had decided to take some time off before continuing on with her education. She was working at a retail store while trying to figure out what she wanted to do with her life. Bob found a part-time job at a warehouse. He also gave guitar lessons and played in a local band on Saturday nights. He hadn't made it yet as a musician, but he would. It was only a matter of time.

A draft had been implemented at this point and the Shields family knew that Bob could be called up at any time. Mr. Shields had served in the military during the Korean War and made no bones about the fact that he expected Bob to do his part as well.

Protests were happening all over the country as those against the U.S. involvement in the war took to the streets to voice their opposition. Bob and Margie weren't the types to join in publicly, but they did have their own opinions. Margie says that they spoke about the events erupting around them in private many times. They were both against the war for various reasons. Margie told her brother how much she worried for him.

For Bob's part, he seemed oddly at peace with the whole thing. He told her that he had even thought of enlisting to ease the anxiety of waiting to be called up. There was no telling how long this mess would go on and he hated having the draft hanging over his head. He reasoned that not everyone died in a war. He told her that, if he enlisted, he could get his service over with and get on with his life. She thought he was kidding.

No one was more surprised than Margie when her brother announced to the family that he had followed through and joined the service. He would be sent to Louisiana for basic training. He knew that there was a good chance that he would go to Vietnam but, there was also the possibility that he would never see combat. He was willing to roll the dice. Unfortunately, he lost.

Bob stayed stateside for several months as the war raged on. When the call came that he was being deployed, it wasn't completely unexpected. The Shields family was devastated, just the same. Their beloved son and brother, who had never harmed a fly, would be going off to war. Margie couldn't believe then, or now, that such a thing would ever happen.

The family heard from Bob only sporadically following his deployment. They wrote to him often, but weren't always sure that he got their letters. They received word from him every so often that he was okay. He wrote that he hated the weather, the bugs, the food and just about everything else involved in his situation at the time. He was counting the days until he could return home and resume his life right where it had left off. For Bob, his time in the Army was just a temporary interruption that would soon pass.

Weeks would go by with no word from Bob. Just when the family would begin to fear that something terrible had happened to him, a letter would arrive allowing them to breathe again. That had been the pattern ever since he had left the states. And then, all at once, the letters ceased entirely.

Margie and her parents waited and waited for some word from Bob. They contacted every agency they could think of in an attempt to get some information about Bob, but no one seemed able to help them. All they could do, for the time being was to wait and hope to hear from him.

To this day, Margie isn't entirely sure if she heard anyone say exactly what became of her brother. She does know that two men came to the family home one evening and that the news they were bearing was not good. One was in uniform and one wasn't. She saw them, but can't remember hearing what was said. She didn't need to hear, she already knew that they were telling her parents that Bob was gone.

The men stayed for a while and sat with her devastated mother and father. Margie didn't want to be around them. She went to her room and closed the door. She remembers sitting in the dark thinking about all of the times she and Bob had spent in that very room talking about their futures. Now, at least for Bob, those dreams were shattered. Even in the solitude of her bedroom, she could still hear muffled voices and the sound of her mother weeping.

Margie would find out later that, although Bob was killed in action, his body had not been recovered. They would end up burying an empty casket. Nothing about the situation seemed real and decades later, she still grapples with the chain of events that led to the loss of her brother.

The surviving members of the Shields family dealt with Bob's death in different ways. Her father, who had been so proud of his boy for making the decision to enlist, rarely spoke of his only son. If anyone around him brought up the subject of Bob, Mr. Shields would excuse himself from the room. They quickly learned that it was best to keep their thoughts to themselves.

Even though Bob was a painful topic in the house, his memory was honored in several ways. The most prominent one was in the form of a large framed photograph that hung in the living room. It was a still shot of Bob just after he completed basic training. The photo showed him in his uniform. It was the last picture, as far as they knew, that had been taken of Bob.

It was a little over a month after they had learned that Bob had been killed that the family began experiencing some odd phenomena. The first thing that Margie remembers is hearing the sound of a guitar playing in the middle of the night.

At first, Margie thought that she was dreaming when the strumming sound would make its way into her room. It was only when it happened a second time that she realized it was not in her head. She jumped up and ran to Bob's room, half expecting to find him there, sitting cross legged on the bed cradling his guitar. That, of course, was not the case. The room was dark and empty, just as it had been since the day that Bob had said goodbye for the last time.

Night after night, Margie would lie in her bed, wide awake, and listen to someone in the next room playing the same song over and over again on an acoustic guitar. She had stopped running to the next room in an effort to catch this mysterious musician in the act. She knew that no one would be there. She wasn't sure if what she was hearing was real or if she was just reliving the past, but it comforted her and became something that she looked forward to.

Margie didn't tell her parents about the nightly guitar playing, though she isn't sure why. It was a secret that she kept to herself for years. Only after her father passed away did she mention it to her mother. It was then that she learned that her mother had heard the same thing, on a nightly basis for months after Bob died. She wasn't sure, but she thought that her husband must have heard it, too.

Another thing that everyone in the family was aware of--and this was no secret--was the fact that someone kept taking the photograph of Bob in his uniform off of the wall and placing it, faced down, on the floor. At first, they would accuse one and other of moving the treasured reminder of Bob. They each denied touching the picture. Still, it would be removed time and time again, even when no one had been in the house.

Bob's favorite food had always been peanut butter and jelly sandwiches. No matter how fancy a meal his mother would prepare, he would usually opt for the old standby. He had been that way since he was a child. His parents had given up long ago trying to change his eating habits. He had always been strong willed, even as a youngster.

Margie and her mother began to notice that someone was leaving a knife in the sink, sometimes more than one time a day, with peanut butter smeared on it. It was a small thing, but still significant because only Margie ate peanut butter. Her father didn't like it and her mother never ate it. Only Margie and Bob had ever eaten it and one of them was gone now. Margie ate a peanut sandwich on occasion, but not regularly. Still, the dirty knife would appear almost every day without explanation.

Bob wasn't with them physically, but so many things suggested that he was still, somehow, in the house. Margie would hear the floor in the hallway creak during the night, a sound she had heard since childhood. She and her brother were the only ones who slept upstairs. She had listened to the familiar creaking as he would get up during the night to go to the bathroom or get a snack, since they were kids. Her parents never came upstairs after they went to bed, there would have been no need.

At any rate, someone was walking around outside her door at night, even though she was the only one left upstairs. This would go on regularly, just like the guitar playing, for several months after Bob passed away. Eventually, the sounds became sporadic and then faded altogether. The memory, however, remains with Margie to this day.

The family had kept Bob's bedroom just as it had been when he still lived there for several years after his death. When they first received news of his death, no one could bring themselves to go through his things. After a while, they simply kept the door closed. It was only after Mr. Shields passed away that Margie and her mother finally got around to sorting through Bob's possessions. It was only then that they realized fully how much Bob had sacrificed.

They discovered that Bob had been much more opposed to the war than they had known. He had collected dozens of newspaper clippings and magazine articles that were strongly against the U.S. involvement. He had kept a journal documenting his own opposition to any sort of conflict. He had been a pacifist through and through and yet he had voluntarily gone to war knowing he might not make it home alive. The more she learned about her brother, the more he fascinated Margie.

Bob had owned a vast collection of literature that revealed that he was, at heart, a philosopher. Most of the books were way beyond anything that Margie could comprehend. She had always thought that Bob was the smart one in the family, but it wasn't until now that she really grasped what that meant. She was also surprised that she had not taken note of his interests while he was still living. She supposed that there hadn't been any pressing need at the time. She hadn't known then that their time together would be cut short.

When all was said and done, most of Bob's things were put right back where they had been found. Neither woman could bring themselves to throw anything away. Her mother told Margie that she would keep the room just as it had been all these years until the time came for her to leave this earth and join her husband and Bob.

By then, Margie was living in her own home with her husband Steven. She understood her mother's decision and supported her. She did ask if she could have a few of Bob's things and her mother agreed. Margie knew that she wanted the one thing that was closest to her brother's heart—his guitar.

The sister Bob left behind still wonders if her brother tried to send the family messages before he moved on to whatever awaited him in the afterlife. After reading some of the materials he had saved regarding the war, she thinks she understands what he was trying to say.

Margie came to believe that it had been Bob who was taking down the framed portrait of him in his uniform. She feels that it was his way of saying that he didn't wish to be remembered that way. In the end, he was a musician at heart, not a soldier and he wanted them to know that. With this in mind, she persuaded her mother to retire the photo. They replaced it with one of Margie's favorite pictures of her brother. It showed Bob, sitting on the floor, playing his guitar. He was deep in concentration and, seemingly, lost in whatever song he was sharing with them. Margie felt that it was a much better representation of her brother. It hung on the living room wall, undisturbed, for the remainder of the time that Margie's mother lived in the house.

Knowing how thoughtful her brother had been, Margie also thinks that the nightly guitar playing was meant to comfort the family in his absence. If so, it worked. Margie missed hearing the bedtime serenade when it ended, but she knew then that she would be okay. Bob was ready to move on and so was she. She took solace in the fact that her brother had, at least for a time, found his way back home.

Chapter 8:
The Dream Man

The following story is one that is a bit difficult to classify. Whether it has its roots in the supernatural is up for debate. In any event, it is strange in so many ways that it definitely has a place in this book. It also begs the question: at what point do our dreams cross the line and enter into the world of reality?

It's been said that we cannot dream of someone whom we have never seen, in some way or another, while we were awake. It could be a stranger we passed on the street and barely took notice of or someone we know well. Whatever the circumstances, we committed their face to our memory, whether we realized it or not.

Angela Williams was not someone who grew up dreaming of meeting her Prince Charming. Instead, she had focused on her one true love—photography—ever since she could remember. She was career oriented and wanted to travel the world, documenting her journeys along the way. She wasn't opposed to finding a partner but, she wasn't looking for one either.

Growing up in Portland, Oregon, Angela had led what she considered a normal life. She was one of four children raised by an engineer and an elementary school teacher. She had never had any experiences that she thought were particularly odd or out of the ordinary until she was in her early twenties. That's when the dreams began that would, in a way, foretell her future.

The first dream hadn't meant much to Angela at the time. She did, however, remember it vividly. She had been trying to climb up a snow-covered hill, but couldn't find her footing. From out of nowhere, a man appeared and took her by the hand. He guided her up the steep hillside until she was safely at the top.

As she thanked the man for his help, she was taken by his kind eyes and gentle smile. She didn't know who he was or where he had come from, but his presence had given her an immediate sense of well-being. Angela woke up before she had the chance to speak with him.

The dream had stayed with Angela for the rest of the day. She couldn't get over how realistic it had been. She felt that she had connected, somehow, with someone who only existed in her imagination. As silly as the notion was to her, she couldn't shake the feeling that it had actually happened.

Days went by and the dream slowly faded from Angela's memory. That is, until the man made another appearance while she was sleeping. This time, Angela was lost in a city she couldn't identify. All she knew was that she was panicking and no one would help her.

As she made her way through the streets of the unknown city, she stumbled and fell onto the sidewalk. As she sat on the pavement, feeling hopeless and alone, a hand reached out to her. When she raised her head to look at whoever was offering their much needed assistance, she recognized the face before her. The man who had guided her up the snowy hill was, once again, offering his aid.

Angela took his outstretched hand and the man lifted her to her feet. His smile immediately put her at ease. She no longer felt lost or desperate. Even in her dream state, Angela remembers telling herself that this was the same man she had seen before. She wanted to ask him his name, but the sound of her alarm clock spoiled the moment. She woke up feeling, although it was impossible, that the encounter had been real.

She isn't sure how many times the mysterious man showed up in her dreams. She still had nights that he didn't appear. She also had dreams that he played no part in. Even so, the man who had no significance in her waking life became a mainstay in her dream world for over a year.

Angela told several of her friends about the man who she knew only in her dreams. Most of them guessed that it was just her subconscious telling her that she was lonely and needed someone in her life.

Angela had thought the same thing. Since the man always showed up to help her when no one else would, maybe it was her mind's way of saying that she felt helpless and needed a partner in life. She knew that it was probably all psychological in nature, but she honestly didn't feel that she needed saving. At least, not while she was awake.

The dreams were still occurring, but not nearly as often, when Angela decided to take a job working as a staff photographer for a large architectural firm in Seattle, Washington. She would be doing what she loved most and earning a sizable salary to boot. She would miss Portland and all of the memories she had made there, but this was an opportunity she couldn't pass up.

Angela quickly adjusted to life in her new home city. She had always made friends easily and it was no time at all before she began socializing with people in her building. She would stop and talk to her neighbors whenever she could. It would be a chance meeting with one resident of the complex that would change her life forever.

One day, when she was checking her mailbox before heading to work, Angela noticed one of the other tenants standing with his back to her. She made it a habit of saying hello to everyone she met in the building, so she smiled and offered a greeting. When the man turned around and smiled back at her, she recognized his face immediately.

She isn't sure, but Angela thinks that the shock must have shown on her face because the man's smile turned to concern right away. He asked her if everything was alright. Once she came to her senses, they spoke briefly and introduced themselves. Most of the brief conversation they shared is lost in Angela's memory. She did recall one important detail—his name. The man she knew instantly as the person from her dreams was Bryan Miller.

Angela and Bryan began to run into each other more and more often around their building. Whether these meetings were by accident or design, she isn't sure and it didn't matter. The more she talked to her fellow tenant, the more she liked him. He was a nice guy and the more she knew of him, the more apparent it became that he was someone she wanted to get to know on a personal level.

Bryan must have felt the same way. He asked Angela out for coffee which turned into them spending the day together. They began dating a short time later. After they had been together as a couple for several months, Angela finally got up the nerve to tell Bryan that she had dreamed about him while she was still living in Portland.

Her new boyfriend, the man she knew before she met him, simply laughed at the bizarre story. Angela had thought that maybe there was a chance that they had shared the dreams, but that was not the case. Bryan reasoned that, perhaps, Angela had run into him on a previous trip to Seattle and remembered his face. She knew that this scenario was unlikely. She hadn't been to Seattle for years prior to the first dream. Still, it was possible.

Angela doesn't know how she dreamed of Bryan so many times before actually meeting him. In the end, it didn't really matter. They dated for over a year and knew that they were meant to be together. They were married in 2008 and have only grown closer with the passage of time.

In the end, whether it was by the hand of destiny, coincidence or chance two people had found each other and built a life together. Angela still calls Bryan the man of her dreams and that he is—in more ways than one.

Chapter 9:
A Child's Place

Many stories come my way that relate the experiences people have had living in houses that showed clear signs of being haunted. The occurrences that take place within these homes are, at times, so similar that they would give pause to even the most steadfast skeptic. The account you are about to read has all of the earmarks of possible paranormal activity. There are, perhaps, logical explanations for the bizarre events this family experienced. What those are, well, that's for someone else to know.

The source of this tale of a presumably haunted house is an acquaintance from the days when I sold real estate named Emily Kerns. It's a story that she had heard many times over the years and passed it on to me when she learned that I was investigating and writing about unexplained phenomena. The events unfolded around her husband and the house in which he grew up. It is a strange tale, indeed.

According to Emily, her husband Craig had grown up in a town called Belle, West Virginia. He was the eldest of three children. His father had worked as a house painter while his mother stayed home and took care of Craig and his siblings. He described his upbringing as impoverished. The house they lived in had no heat in the winter and no source of air in the blistering summer. Still, since it was all they had ever known, they managed to get by.

The family had never had any dealings with the supernatural until an act of nature destroyed their ramshackle home and they were forced to move into a new house across town. It was there, in their upgraded lodgings, that their resolve would be tested and all that they had known previously about fantasy and reality would be thrown to the wind.

After the family lost their home, members of the church they attended stepped up to help them find a new place to live. The new house was larger and nicer than the one they had lived in previously. They would now enjoy true warmth in the winter for the very first time.

Almost immediately upon moving in, Craig remembers that something wasn't right with the house. The first indication that they might not be alone came when doors began flying open and slamming shut when no one was touching them.

On at least one occasion, he says that every door in the house shut with a loud band at exactly the same time. Even his father, who didn't believe in ghosts or anything of the like, half-jokingly proclaimed that he thought there was a "spook" in the house.

The thing that Craig remembered the most, and the one that most terrified him, was the time when he was jolted from sleep by his bed shaking so violently that it was actually moving across the floor with him on it. He was so paralyzed with fear that he stayed on the bed, afraid that if he jumped off, whatever was moving it would turn its attention to him. Instead, he covered his head with the blanket and prayed over and over until the bed came to rest across the room from where it had should have been.

Craig knew that what had happened was not his imagination when, the following morning, his father asked him why he had been making such a racket during the night. His parents had heard the thumping noises from their room, but hadn't been concerned enough at the time to investigate. The thought that some unseen force was at work in their home was still a subject they considered laughable.

The child who seemed to have the most contact with whatever was sharing the house with them was Craig's youngest sister. She was only four at the time so no one took much of what she said seriously. If they had, they might have given more stock to the notion that they were living in a house that was already occupied by something not of this world that they could neither identify nor imagine.

The little girl often talked about the playmates she had in the house. There was not just one, but several entities that occupied the child's time. She called them by silly names that no one seems to be able to remember. According to her, they were both grownups and children. She was never afraid of them and they had neither threatened nor harmed her. She did say, quite often, that they didn't like anyone else in the house. The words they used were not, however, that benign.

It became apparent, as time passed, that someone wanted everyone, except for the youngest child, to get out of the house. This became clear to Craig when other family members began to fall victim to accidents and injuries that they couldn't explain.

Craig's mother had fallen over backwards one day while in the laundry room. The kids were in the living room when they heard her screams. When they found her, she was lying on the floor. Her face was as white as a sheet. She had no explanation for how she had ended up flat on her back. All she knew was that she had been minding her own business when she felt something, that she could not see, hit her full on in the chest. Years later, she told her son that she had nursed a large bruise just below her collarbone for weeks following the incident.

The other children in the house also suffered odd injuries at the hands of something unknown to them. Kids fall and get hurt all of the time in the course of playing, but this was different. Craig would wake up with angry red marks on his arms that had no reason to be there. His younger brother fell, not once but, twice while getting out of the bathtub. Both times, he claimed that something had grabbed his leg as he had tried to step out of the tub. He wasn't seriously injured, but he did sport bruises on his shins after the falls.

Craig's father seemed to be the only one who wasn't bothered by accidents in the home. If he had been, he didn't share it with his family. A practical man, it would have been out of character for him to admit that the house was haunted. As so many people in these situations do, he opted to pretend it wasn't happening. Sometimes, that's all one can do.

As all of this was going on, the little girl still spoke daily of her friends in the house. She chattered away with them just as she did with the members of her real family. Sometimes, she would surprise her parents or brothers by telling them that her friends didn't like them. She would laugh about it even as she told them that such and such really wanted them to go away and die.

It was after spending two years in the house that the family situation finally changed. It was then that Craig's grandfather died. The news, as sad as it was, turned out to be a blessing for the family. They soon learned that, in his will, he had bequeathed them his house in Charleston, West Virginia.

Only the youngest child was upset to be leaving the house. On the day they packed up the last of their belongings, Craig says she screamed and cried as they carried her out the front door. He had never seen her so upset. The youngster cried so hard that she couldn't catch her breath. Even as they drove away, she pressed her face against the car's window and sobbed. She didn't want to leave her friends behind.

As disturbing a scene as that had been for the family, and as traumatized as his sister had seemed, the atmosphere changed completely as soon as the house was out of sight and she immediately calmed down. Maybe it was because small children get over things quickly. Or, perhaps, whatever hold the otherworldly residents of the house had over the girl was broken once she was out of their grasp. Who knows?

The family had no further incidents once they moved into their new home. Whatever had been haunting them was, apparently, attached to the dwelling instead of the people who lived there. Craig's little sister, who had been so close to her "friends" in the old house, never spoke of them again.

Chapter 10:
Only What the Eyes Can See

The phenomenon of people seeing visions of things that occurred in the past are one curiosity I don't often come across. There are only two that stand out in my mind. One was submitted to me on social media. The other is a little known account that involved an actress who became known more for the events surrounding her brutal murder than the body of her work. They are both terrifying in their own right.

Mary Laughlin's family moved around quite a bit during her formative years. It was in a house that they rented in Annandale, Virginia that she saw something she can't explain. Before her very eyes, she witnessed a murder as it was taking place. Making it all the more shocking, she was the only one in the room at the time.

Mary estimates that she was around eleven years old when she had her encounter with the supernatural. It was sometime around New Year's, 1993. She had gotten up during the night and decided to go to the kitchen to find something to snack on. Before she made it into the room, she could tell that someone was already there.

The way the house was set up, one had to walk through the dining room to get to the kitchen. A large archway separated the two rooms, but there was no door. As she neared the entrance to the kitchen, she could see the images of two men standing in the middle of the floor. One of the men was talking to the other, but no words were coming out of his mouth. The room was silent.

Mary described the scene as looking like something out of an old movie. She could see the men well enough to describe their faces and clothing, even though they seemed to be cast in a sort of grainy film that made it apparent that they were not really there. Mary was also aware that, even though she could see them, they could not see her.

Despite her young age at the time, she didn't scream or cry out when she found the men in her family's home. They didn't seem real to her. Instead, she stood silently and watched as they interacted with each other. She only began to feel fear when she saw that one of the men had a weapon.

Mary isn't sure what the man was holding in his hand. Whatever it was, he raised it over his head and struck the other man several times causing him to fall to the floor. Again, there was complete silence in the room. A horribly violent event was taking place right in front of her, but she couldn't hear a sound. It was as if she was watching a reel from a silent movie, except that this was playing out in real time right in front of her.

As she watched, the man who was still standing continued to strike the man on the floor over and over again with the implement he was wielding. Mary knew that, when he finally stopped and threw the weapon onto the floor, the other man was dead. She could see a pool of liquid all around his head. Even though everything involving the men was devoid of color, she knew that the substance was blood.

Still unable to move or scream, she stood helplessly watching as the killer and his victim began to fade from her vision. In a matter of seconds, they were gone. There was not a drop of blood on the floor, or anywhere else in the room. It was as if it had never happened. Everything in the room went back to normal.

No longer in the mood to eat, Mary retreated to her room. She remembers lying in bed the rest of the night thinking about what she had witnessed in the kitchen. She had seen a murder take place involving two men she didn't know. It had not been a dream. She had been walking around and wide awake. She didn't know if she should tell anyone or not. She waited until morning to make that decision.

She ended up telling her mother the whole story of what she had seen in the kitchen. Just as she had feared, her mom told her that she had experienced a nightmare. Her mother assured her that it had only seemed real. The subject was changed and the matter dropped. Mary saw the spectral murder only once while living in the house. To her knowledge, no one else in the family ever witnessed anything out of the ordinary.

Even though her mother didn't believe her story, other people she has confided in over the years did. She has since become convinced that she had borne witness to a crime that had occurred sometime in the past. Perhaps the violent scene had played itself out every night without anyone's knowledge. Mary had simply been the unfortunate one who stumbled upon it before the final act was completed. Energy tends to repeat itself, especially if it is tied to a particularly heinous event.

Mary does not know who the men were that she saw in the kitchen that night. Judging by their outdated clothing and slicked back hair, she thinks that they probably lived decades before she was even born. One thing she is certain of is that they had been actual living beings at some point and that one had killed the other. Whether it had taken place in the house or in a dwelling that existed there prior to the house being built, she doesn't know. She does know that she will forever be tied to them, having been a witness to murder.

Another story which follows similar lines is that of actress Sharon Tate. Her experience was even more chilling and, sadly, may have been an indicator of the horrifying fate that awaited her in the future.

Sharon Tate was a Texas beauty queen before she ended up in Hollywood. Although she would land roles in several films and television series', it would be in death that she would be immortalized.

In 1967, Sharon was dating a popular men's hair stylist named Jay Sebring. He had already made a name for himself as one of the most sought after stylists in the film industry. He boasted many celebrity clients by the time he met the young starlet. They were a striking couple who fit in perfectly with the Hollywood elite.

One night, while Jay was in New York, Sharon stayed at his house in Benedict Canyon. It was the first time that she had been in the house alone. She would later recall hearing strange noises during the night that made it difficult for her to fall asleep.

She claimed that, besides the unidentified noises, she had also seen a man aimlessly wandering around her bedroom. It was dark, but she knew from pictures she had seen previously that the man was one of the home's previous tenants, a man by the name of Paul Bern.

Bern had been married to Hollywood siren Jean Harlow in the 1930s. The union had not lasted and the couple split up in 1932. It was said that Bern was so distraught after the break up that he shot himself in the house. There had always been some doubt as to whether his death was by his own hand or if foul play was involved. In any event, no one disputes the fact that he died in the house in which Jay Sebring now resided.

Sharon went on to say that she was acutely aware of everything going on around her in the bedroom. She didn't think that she was dreaming, it all seemed too real. Even though the man in the room with her hadn't taken any notice of the young woman lying in the bed, she suddenly felt the need to run away.

Mustering up her nerve, Sharon bolted out of the bed and ran out of the room. As she reached the staircase that led to the main floor of the house, she froze at the ghastly sight before her. There, tied to the banister, was the body of someone who had been horribly brutalized.

Sharon related that she knew, instinctively, that the person was either Jay or herself. Chillingly, whichever it was, their throat had been flayed open and blood gushed from the gaping wound.

In a panic, Sharon ran past the body and down the stairs. In her frazzled state, she searched for something to calm her nerves. Unfamiliar with the house, she couldn't seem to locate where Jay kept his liquor cabinet.

Although she didn't hear an actual voice, Sharon claimed that someone communicated to her that what she was looking for could be found on a shelf in the bookcase. Sure enough, the liquor supply was just where she had been directed. She proceeded to pour herself a drink.

As she sat nursing her drink, it suddenly occurred to Sharon that she must be dreaming. To test her theory, she pinched herself. Feeling nothing, she assumed that she had been correct. This was just a dream. She would wake up soon and it would all be over.

Even as she convinced herself that she was dreaming, Sharon was once again prompted by an unseen force to peel away the wallpaper on the bar. She obliged and removed bits of paper, revealing the brass plating underneath. She didn't know why she did it or what significance the act could have.

By this time, she had finished her drink and decided to go back upstairs and return to bed. This was odd, since she had assumed that she was sleeping the whole time. Even so, she walked up the stairs and past the body which still sat bound to the staircase.

The man that she had seen earlier roaming around the bedroom was still there as well. He seemed lost and totally oblivious to her and the victim on the stairs. She would later describe the man in the room, whom she thought was Paul Bern, as an "odd little man." Sharon paid him no mind as she crawled into bed and fell asleep.

Early the following morning, Jay Sebring returned home. He woke Sharon who proceeded to tell him all about the bizarre dream that had so distressed her. They discussed her harrowing night for a while before heading downstairs.

When the couple entered the room that Jay referred to as the "playroom", they discovered pieces of wallpaper lying strewn about the floor near the bar. They also noted that the liquor cabinet had been left open. They didn't say it out loud, but they were both thinking the same thing, perhaps Sharon hadn't been dreaming after all.

She and Jay eventually broke up, but remained close friends. Two years after the incident at his house, Sharon was living in the home she shared with her husband, Roman Polanski, in the Hollywood Hills. The address was 10050 Cielo Drive.

At this time, Sharon was eight months pregnant with her first child, a boy she had already named Paul in honor of her father. Her husband was in Europe finishing up a film he was directing while she prepared the house for the new arrival.

Not wanting to be alone in the late stages of her pregnancy, Sharon had asked a few friends to stay in the home with her until Roman returned home. Those friends: Abigail Folger, Voytek Frykowski, and Jay Sebring would all meet their fates one blistering August night, as would Sharon.

I won't go into the grisly details as you're probably already familiar with the murders that sent shockwaves throughout Hollywood and the entire world. It is the visions that Sharon saw two years earlier that leave one to ponder if she might have witnessed, in a way, her own murder.

Sharon had said herself that she felt that the person bound to the banister was either she or Jay. On the night of their actual murders, they had been tied to each other by a cord that had then been suspended from the rafters. They had not, however, been hung. Rather, they had both been slashed and stabbed numerous times.

The "odd little man" that Sharon encountered on the night of her premonition may very well have been the deceased Paul Bern. However, there is the possibility, however remote, that the shadowy figure she witnessed in the bedroom belonged to someone else.

The idea has been put forth that the presence could have been that of the person who would go on to orchestrate the murders of all those unlucky enough to be present at 10050 Cielo Drive on the evening of August 8, 1969. Such a notion would be preposterous if not for one telling detail: Charles Manson, the instigator of Sharon's murder—among others—stood at a diminutive 5'2.

Epilogue

Life's mysteries stretch far and wide. They know no rhyme or reason. One person's reality is another's fantasy. Until one has experienced the extraordinary for themselves, their minds aren't always willing to accept the fact that we are just a small piece of an infinite puzzle. We cannot begin to know all of the forces that are at work around us at all times. Things that we are not meant to see surround us every moment of the day. It is only when worlds intersect and those mysterious other realms come to light, however briefly, that we realize we are not alone. Whether they manifest as hauntings, life-like dreams, premonitions of events yet to come or any of the other countless ways they make their presence known, they are very real to those who encounter them. So, the next time you glimpse a movement out of the corner of your eye or hear a sound that you can't quite identify, don't be so quick to assume that it's only your imagination. It might just be someone, or something's, way of telling you that things you don't dare acknowledge are closer than you think. Remember; just because you don't see them, it doesn't mean that they aren't there.

Acknowledgements

Thank you to all of the people who were kind enough to share their personal stories for this book.

Likewise, thank you to all of the people who read my books. You make it all worthwhile.

*Note that some names have been altered at the request of the contributors.

Sources:

Allison Walters
Holly Young
Sue Burns
Cheryl Simons
Beth Thompson
Carmen Ball
The Sims Family
Judy Santer
Margeret Shields
Angela Williams
Emily Kerns
Mary Laughlin
Sharon Tate's Premonition—Dick Kleiner—*Fate* Magazine
The Tate/LaBianca Murders—*Time* Magazine

True Tales of the Supernatural & Unexplained: Volume 1 is the sole intellectual property of its author Cindy Parmiter

No unauthorized reproduction permitted without author's express written consent.

All rights reserved

Cover art licensed through, and courtesy of alga38

Copyright established: February 2018

Made in the USA
Columbia, SC
05 November 2023